INTERNAL DESECRATION

Traumatization and Representations of God

Carrie Doehring

UNIVERSITY
PRESS OF
AMERICA

Lanham • New York • London

Copyright © 1993 by
University Press of America®, Inc.
4720 Boston Way
Lanham, Maryland 20706

3 Henrietta Street
London WC2E 8LU England

Library of Congress Cataloging-in-Publication Data
Doehring, Carrie.
Internal desecration : traumatization and representations of God /
Carrie Doehring.
p.   cm.
Includes bibliographical references and index.
1. Psychology, Religious.   2. Psychic trauma.
3. God—Attributes.   I. Title.
BL53.D616   1993   291.2'11'019—dc20   93–19029 CIP

ISBN 0–8191–9120–5 (cloth : alk. paper)
ISBN 0–8191–9121–3 (pbk. : alk. paper)

In the aftermath of violence,
when the inner sanctum of being has been desecrated,
we may be blessed with the presence of companions,
who venture with us into the innermost sanctum,
empowering us,
so that we can take on the gods who reign there,
cast them out,
and consecrate again this holiest of places,
God within us.

This book is dedicated to such companions.

ACKNOWLEDGEMENTS

I am indebted to my colleagues at Boston University---Merle Jordan, Carole Bohn and Chris Schlauch---for encouragement, support, laughter, and astute criticism.

Joshua Wootton's work, developing the God representation tasks, was a model of scholarly research which inspired this study.

I am grateful to Don Doehring, my father, for his help with research design and statistical analyses. Working together was an opportunity to appreciate his considerable gifts as a teacher and research methodologist.

I am appreciative of those who listened and offered emotional, intellectual and spiritual support, day in and day out: Carol Wintermeyer and Susan Adelman.

Finally, I am thankful for my husband, Mark Jones, a fellow companion on the way, and our sons, Jordan and Alex, who daily remind us that the innocence of childhood is a cherished garden: a delight to behold, a sacred space to nurture and protect.

TABLE OF CONTENTS

CHAPTER THREE: METHODOLOGY 53

CHAPTER FOUR: RESULTS 59

LIST OF TABLES

LIST OF FIGURES

INTRODUCTION

> Do you not know that you are God's temple and that God's spirit dwells in you? ... For God's temple is holy, and that temple you are. (1 Cor. 3:16-17)

A woman from the former Soviet Union recently described to me how she grew up in a country where places of worship, the Russian Orthodox churches of her people, were often abandoned, falling into disrepair, or had been converted into warehouses. She commented that often such churches were in the background in her dreams, sentinels on the horizon of her consciousness, and indeed the consciousness of her people, of a faith that had been abandoned.

The place within, where we seek God and God awaits us is a sacred place, like churches within our interior landscape. It is our embodiment of the goodness of creation, the goodness of being made, male and female, in the image of God. When our very beings are violated, through physical and sexual violence, this is a desecration of the inner sanctuary.

We can imagine the churches within the interior landscape of the violated child. In the moment of violence, the church doors are ripped open, intruders enter and begin smashing the sacred symbols, defacing the icons of inner saints. They smash the stained glass windows. The bright sunshine of noonday is no longer refracted into rays of light that shine within. When inner lights burn at dusk, the brilliant colors of the windows no longer glow. The altar is overturned, the food scattered, the vessels broken. The sacristy lamp is shattered, extinguishing the light, plunging the inner sanctuary into darkness. Such is the desecration of the inner temple when violence strikes.

Such desecration may be temporary, in the immediate experience of violence and the acute response to violence that follows. When love surrounds the violated child and caring empathic adults step in to restore safety, respond to confusion, fear, anger and shame, then the inner temple can be repaired and reconsecrated in such moments of love. When neglect follows violence, then the inner temple remains desecrated, derelict, occupied by squatters: the inner representations formed in the traumatic experience and its aftermath. These are the inner voices that invoke shame and fear, and reign like gods in the inner world of the child, and later the adult.

The images of the inner sanctuary, trauma as desecration, healing as a restoration and reconsecration: this is the poem, indeed the prayer beneath the technical language of this research project. I invite the reader to hear these images as ever present throughout this text, like a hymn, that becomes the foundation of a chorale prelude; sounded out, over and over again, sometimes in bass notes so low that we do not actually hear them but feel them. In presenting this poem at the outset, I am disclosing some of the deep metaphors which shape my understanding of childhood abuse. These metaphors at times may enhance and deepen my discussion and conclusions; at other times, they may distort my reflections, in that I may twist and shape interpretations that are dissonant with my metaphors. Browning (1991) emphasizes the importance of practicing hermeneutical psychological research in which one is aware of the metaphors and assumptions one brings to research, acknowledging that one cannot be neutral and objective.

It is easy, in doing research, and indeed, doctoral studies, to lose the poem/prayer that seeded our ideas, energized studies, and made the tedious details bearable. When our work is over, we may look upon what we have done like some valley of old bones. Holding onto the poem, rediscovering it in times when it becomes forgotten, is like breathing life into the old bones, such that they become alive, and take up their dance again. I hope that in publishing this research, I can model ways for us to explore the deep, troubling questions we have, that come out of our relationships and our concern for each other. I hope that we can hold onto the poem/prayer inherent in our questions, and learn to ask and answer these questions in the many discourses available to us, including that of quantitative research.

In the opening chapter of this book I state the research problem I wanted to explore: the inter-relationship between childhood/adolescent experiences of abuse and women's adult images of God. The terms, severity of traumatization and mental representations of God, are elaborated in exploring this research problem.

In the second chapter I review four major bodies of literature: 1) psychodynamic models of traumatization, 2) empirical measures of traumatization, 3) the origins and development of mental representations of God, and 4) empirical measures of God representations. The overlap of the literature on psychodynamic models of traumatization and mental representations of God is like the ground of an excavation site. Upon this ground I sketch what I expect to find as I dig. This sketch is the structural model of personality I develop, describing the way core metaphors of God and self are the deep structure of the personality. These core metaphors give rise to cognitive schemata: the belief systems describing who God is, who we are, and how we understand the world. What I expect to find, as I dig, is this: at the deepest level of personality, there is a powerful interaction between traumatization and God representations, such that, as traumatization increases, loving and observing God representations decrease, while absent and wrathful God representations increase. In the survey of empirical measures of traumatization and God representations, I explore the tools I will use to measure the hypothesized inter-relationship between traumatization and mental representations of God.

In the third chapter, I set forth the research design, describing the sample, the instrumentation, procedures and statistical analyses undertaken. In the fourth chapter I outline the statistical findings: the significant negative correlation between traumatization and loving representations of God, and the significant positive correlations between traumatization and absent and wrathful representations of God. These findings are elucidated in a further statistical analysis, when the sample group is divided into four trauma groups, based on scores from the Traumatic Antecedents Questionnaire: no trauma, trauma, high trauma and severe trauma.[1] When the God representations of these four trauma groups are compared, there is no significant difference between loving God, absent God and wrathful God representation scores for the first three trauma groups: no trauma, trauma, and high trauma. It is only when traumatization is severe, that loving, absent and wrathful God scores become significantly different.

In the fifth chapter, these findings are interpreted, using the three psychodynamic models of traumatization, and the structural model describing the inter-relationship between traumatization and God representations. I describe how the quantitative truth of the research findings can be placed along side the metaphorical truth of psychodynamic models, and how we can describe the resonance or dissonance between quantitative findings and metaphorical models. A simple interpretation of the major finding of this study which is dissonant with all three psychodynamic models is that traumatization in childhood is not inter-related with one's God representations in adulthood unless it is severe. A more complex conclusion which is consonant with all three models has to do with differences in simple and complex post-traumatic stress disorder, repression, self-fragmentation, the capacity to repair or reconstruct representations of God in the aftermath of traumatization, and the societal pressures on victims of abuse to maintain representations of God and parents as loving. The finding is elaborated by interfacing Herman's (1992, p. 121) model of complex post-traumatic stress disorder and Spero's (1992, p. 141) model of external objects, anthropocentric and deocentric God representations.

Included in a discussion of the significance of the findings is a discussion of secondary findings, limitations of the study and areas of further research. In the sixth chapter, I describe the research and clinical significance of the findings, as well as the significance of the findings for the community of faith.

---

[1]"No trauma" actually means no conscious memories of trauma, since the Traumatic Antecedents Questionnaire measures women's conscious memories of childhood experiences.

CHAPTER ONE

THE INTER-RELATIONSHIP BETWEEN TRAUMATIZATION AND GOD REPRESENTATIONS

Statement of the Problem

Is there an inter-relationship between experiences of childhood and adolescent abuse, and the way women as adults consciously describe God? Specifically, as experiences of sexual abuse, physical abuse and witnessing domestic violence increase in childhood and adolescence, do women as adults consciously experience God as less loving and observing, and more absent and wrathful? A methodological question is, can this relationship be measured quantitatively? A definition of the terms, severity of traumatization and types of God representations, elaborates the questions posed.

Definitions

Severity of Traumatization

Psychic traumatization is the intrapsychic response to an acute or chronic life-threatening traumatic stressor, such as combat, physical or sexual abuse[1] or assault, and natural disasters (hurricanes, floods, tornadoes, earthquakes).[2]

---

[1]In a review of empirical literature on child sexual abuse, Kendall-Tackett, Meyer Williams and Finkelhor (1993, p. 174) note that "much sexual abuse, however, lacks these components [overwhelming, sudden and dangerous], especially abuse that occurs through manipulation of the child's affections and misrepresentation of social standards."

[2]Herman (1992, p. 33) notes that when post-traumatic stress disorder was first defined, life-threatening stressors like sexual and domestic violence were thought of as outside the range of ordinary life experience. With increasing disclosure of violence, we realize how common such

Traumatic stressors are external events. Psychic traumatization is the internal affect state, the psychological response to the traumatic stressors.[3]

The terms, traumatic stressors, traumatization, and severity of traumatization can be described metaphorically. A traumatic stressor is like an earthquake: an external event with potential for great destruction. Traumatization can be likened to the effect of an earthquake on a house, where the house is an image of the personality. Severity of traumatization describes the degree of damage done to the personality, like the damage done to a house in an earthquake. Damage can range from seemingly no external signs of damage, to structural damage, to the complete destruction of the house.[4]

Van der Kolk (1987, pp. 10-12) has proposed that _severity of traumatization_ depends on six factors. The first is the severity of the traumatic stressor. The more horrific the traumatic stressor is, the more severe the traumatization will be. Extermination camps and exposure to atomic bombing, such as happened in the second World War, are examples of extreme traumatic stressors.[5] The more life-threatening the stressor, the greater the degree of violence, and the longer the duration of exposure to the stressor, the greater the internal traumatization will be. There is a spectrum of traumatic stressors that range from circumscribed traumatic stressors to prolonged, repeated traumatic stressors. Herman (1992, pp.119-122) has suggested a corresponding spectrum of post-traumatic stress disorders, ranging from simple to complex traumatization.

A second factor influencing the severity of traumatization is genetic predisposition. In animal studies of learned helplessness (Maier & Seligman, 1976), one third of the dogs did not develop a response of "learned helplessness" when exposed to situations in which they could not escape noxious stimuli. This suggests that genetic factors may account for the differences from animal to animal. Genetic factors are one of the conditions that can predispose a child to abuse (Friedrich & Boriskin, 1976), with prematurity, mental retardation, and physical handicaps as other factors. Green (1978, p. 93), in a study of 20 abused

---

stressors are.

[3]In the literature, the term, trauma, can refer to both the traumatic stressor and to the state of psychic traumatization. Lindy (1986, pp. 197-198) makes the distinction between traumatic stressors as external events and psychic traumatization as the internal response.

[4]Shengold (1989) uses the image, soul murder, to describe the destruction of personality structures caused by severe traumatic stressors.

[5]While these traumatic stressors may be categorized on a continuum from mild to severe, it is crucial to recognize that 1) the internal response to a traumatic stressor is idiosyncratic and 2) efforts to quantify traumatization by quantifying traumatic stressors may equate the external event (the traumatic stressor) with the internal event (the idiosyncratic intrapsychic response). In such an equation the complexity of the intrapsychic response is lost.

children, found that "deviant psychological and constitutional endowment of the child often complemented the pathological environment as a crucial variable associated with abuse." Constitutional endowment might play a role in a child being singled out as the one who is "a scapegoat and [is] perceived as the major source of the family's frustrations" (Green, 1978, p. 93).

A third factor influencing the severity of traumatization is the developmental phase in which traumatization is experienced. Van der Kolk (1987, p. 11) notes that "children are thought to be extraordinarily sensitive to the long-term effects of uncontrollably traumatic events." Research on traumatization in children supports this conclusion (Terr, 1979, 1983; Green, 1983; Finkelhor, 1984). Child abuse may be further compounded by "a background of poverty, family disorganization, and an interruption of maternal care, resulting in early experiences of object loss and emotional deprivation" (Green, 1978, p. 93). Age can also be a factor in the severity of traumatization further along in the life cycle. Research with combat veterans highlights the way in which younger soldiers were more likely to be severely traumatized than older soldiers (Hendin, Pollinger Haas, Singer et al., 1983; Hendin & Pollinger Haas, 1984; Laufer, Brett & Gallops, 1984; Laufer, Frey-Wouters & Gallops, 1985).

A fourth factor influencing severity of traumatization is the quality of a person's social support system. Social support can be defined as "the degree to which an individual perceives that he or she may rely on one or more people for assistance with either tangible or emotional aid or both in times of need" (Figley & Burge, 1983, p. 2). Figley (1986, p. 40) states that "the family, plus the social support system in general, is the single most important resource to emotional recovery from disaster." An empathic social support system can serve the function of providing psychological support when the defenses and coping mechanisms of the traumatized individual are incapacitated. The loss of such a support system can greatly compound the effects of psychic traumatization (Erikson, 1976; Pynoos & Eth, 1985; Janoff-Bulman, 1985; Krugman, 1987; van der Kolk, 1987). This is especially true of children who have been sexually abused, where the lack of support from caretakers can be as severe a traumatic stressor as the abuse itself (Kobasa & Pucetti, 1982; Green, 1983; Fish-Murray, Koby, & van der Kolk 1987; Doehring, 1987). The term, "sanctuary trauma" describes the further trauma experienced by traumatized people who not only do not receive social support, but are mistreated by the social support systems following traumatization (Silver, 1986).

A fifth factor affecting severity of traumatization is whether individuals have experienced prior traumatization. If prior traumatization has not been worked through, then it may compound the effects of traumatic stressors and increase the severity of psychic traumatization. Exposure to traumatic stressors in childhood has been correlated with the development of post-traumatic stress disorder in combat veterans whose buddies were killed (Lidz, 1946; Fairbairn, 1952). Sometimes early childhood trauma resulted in personality changes such that veterans did not form strong attachments to others. Titchener (1986, p. 18) describes the personality changes that can occur following traumatization as post-traumatic decline, "which results in the removal of the person from meaningful participation in family, society, work, and all forms of gratification." The inter-related effects of factors affecting severity of traumatization can be seen when one considers how personality changes following traumatization can lead to isolation, increasing the likelihood that there will be no social support system.

A final factor influencing severity of traumatization is pre-existing personality: its strengths and weaknesses, its areas of vulnerability and its resources. Van der Kolk (1987, p. 12) notes research indicating that there is a strong relationship between pre-existing personality factors and chronic post-traumatic stress (Brill, 1967; Burgess & Holmstrom, 1974; Horowitz, 1976; Burgess & Holmstrom, 1979). Herman (1992, pp. 58-60) cites several studies that describe how the triad of active, task-oriented coping strategies, strong sociability and internal locus of control characterizes both children and adults who are highly resilient to traumatization. The internal abilities to maintain, even intensify one's social support system, to stay active and focused under stress, and to maintain a sense of empowerment without moving towards being overpowered are all qualities of personality that make individuals less vulnerable to traumatization.

Of these six factors which determine the severity of traumatization, five can be explored through a questionnaire, while the sixth factor, genetic predisposition, cannot. Herman and van der Kolk (1990) have developed the Traumatic Antecedents Questionnaire which gathers information about severity of three specific traumatic stressors: physical abuse, sexual abuse and witnessing domestic violence. The questionnaire also can be used to determine the developmental stage at which these traumatic stressors occurred, the social support system available at the time of traumatization and following traumatization, and prior experiences of sexual abuse, physical abuse and witnessing domestic violence. While pre-existing personality may be inferred through questionnaire data, such an assessment of pre-existing personality is quite limited.

A simple means of quantifying the information gathered in the questionnaire was developed (Herman, Perry & van der Kolk, 1989, p. 491). A score measuring severity of traumatization was derived by counting types of abuse experienced (physical abuse, sexual abuse, and witnessing domestic violence) in each of three developmental stages (childhood, latency and adolescence). Additional scores were added if there was more than one perpetrator.

This scoring procedure allows a simple means of quantifying 1) severity of three specific traumatic stressors compounded by 2) developmental phase, and 3) prior traumatization (when the traumatic stressors are physical abuse, sexual abuse and witnessing domestic violence). This scoring procedure does not measure the degree to which traumatization is compounded by factors such as lack of social support system, pre-existing personality, genetic predisposition, and severity of or prior traumatization by other traumatic stressors (such as emotional abuse and neglect).

Participants answering these questions describe their conscious memories of sexual abuse, physical abuse and witnessing domestic violence. Some individuals who have been traumatized, especially at an early age, may have no conscious memories of these experiences; or some individuals may have recovered some but not all memories of being traumatized. The Traumatic Antecedents Questionnaire is limited to the reporting of conscious memories of traumatic experiences, and the limitations of this will be noted further.

In this exploratory research project the term, severity of traumatization, will be operationally defined as the score yielded when answers to questions about abuse on the Traumatic Antecedents Questionnaire are scored and added together.

God Representation

God representation is the term used to describe conscious and unconscious images of God. A God representation is a type of object representation. The term, object representation, is used by psychodynamic psychologists to describe the way people psychically, or internally, represent someone (the external object) with whom they are in relation.

In forming object representations, the child's raw data is not the external object, per se, but sensations arising from various sources, which form a multitude of impressions, a whole range, for example, of mother images (Sandler & Rosenblatt, 1962, pp. 132-133). In this way, raw sensory data becomes transformed by the child into representations which create meaning:

> Representations are organized compilations of past experiences, relatively enduring impressions, constellations of perceptions and images, which the child culls from his [or her] various experiences and which in turn provide for the child a kind of cognitive map, a subjective landscape within which he [or she] can locate and evoke the cast of characters and events within the drama of his [or her] experience. (Greenberg & Mitchell, 1983, p. 373)

An object representation is an <u>unconscious</u> psychic organization which is the source of the conscious symbols, images, fantasies, thoughts, feelings or actions (Beres & Joseph, 1970). The object representation has a semiotic function (Piaget, 1970). It is the internal signifier which represents that which is signified, that is, the external object.

The God representation is special in that it is both (1) an object of our creation, similar to "fictive creations of our minds---those of creative artists for example" (Rizzuto, 1979, p. 47), and (2) for the believer, "real, existing, alive and interacting...the only relevant object who has not undergone and cannot undergo reality testing" (Rizzuto, 1979, p. 49). Everyone raised within our culture forms precursors[6] of God representations in early childhood, but these may remain static and/or repressed.

The concept of a transitional object was developed by Winnicott (1958) to describe childhood objects, such as a teddy bear or blanket, that are used to navigate the transition from dependence on the caretaker to more independence. Such objects are also transitional representations in that

> [They are] not actually taken to be the mother, and yet are also not fully an abstract symbolic representation of her. [They are] transitional in the movement from concrete representation to the achievement of a true symbol. (Eagle, 1984, p. 194)

Transitional objects are neither wholly internal or external, but rather in between, in what Winnicott calls the transitional space.

God is a "special" transitional object in that God is not an external object, like a teddy bear, who is invested with material from internal representations, like mother, but is an internal object, "whose sources are the representations of primary objects" (Rizzuto, 1979, p. 178), like those of mother and father. Unlike other transitional objects, the God representation is not de-cathected in the process of development. Instead, the meaning of this representation becomes intensified and can evolve as the self evolves. Its meaning is as rich and complex as all of the significant object representations of the internal world.

It is crucial to note the psychologistic assumption underlying Rizzuto's description of God as a transitional object that is wholly internally derived:

---

[6]Spero (1992, p. 72) describes these earliest formations of God representations as precursors, noting that "the formation of the religious paradigm or precursor... is as inevitable as the creation of the first transitional object, though it is not inevitable that it will eventually take the form of God."

God representations themselves, according to this school [the prevailing psychologistic view] are attributed to psychic manufacture rather than any actual form of interchange between a human and a veridically existing divinity. (Spero, 1992, p. 15)

A religionistic assumption is that God representations are not only internally derived but also are externally derived from one's relationship with God. Spero proposes that there are two sources of God representations: interpersonal relationships (an anthropocentric source) and direct or indirect relationships with an objective God (a deocentric source).[7]

Object relations theorists have described the origins and development of God representations (Rizzuto, 1979; Meissner, 1977, 1978, 1984, 1987; McDargh, 1983; Randour & Bondanza, 1987; Spero, 1987, 1992). Meissner (1984, p. 138) takes a developmental approach, describing how the "full range of religious behavior and experience may be conceptualized" within psychoanalytic parameters. He uses a psychodynamic understanding of early childhood development and describes how God representations are part of this development. Rizzuto (1979) uses object relations theory, especially the writings of Winnicott, to describe how God is a transitional object. She studied the God representations of 20 people, using a questionnaire and asking them to draw pictures of God. She describes these God representations in a case study format. McDargh (1983) integrates Fowler's theory on faith development with object relations theory to describe "in a schematic way the various psychological dimensions of faith as a complex structure that underlies the processes of formation of the self" (McDargh, 1983, p. 133). He illustrates the complexity of faith development with two extended case studies, paying particular attention to the interaction between what he calls the "self-becoming" with the object representation of God. Spero (1992) proposes a model of the formation of both anthropocentric and deocentric God representations that includes an objective divine object as part of the external reality. Social and religious schema act as modificatory mechanisms that shape the perception and organization of images, fantasies, thoughts, feelings or actions associated with parents and God (Spero, 1992, p. 139). Projected representations of God and religious schema can be understood as approximations of who God really is; approximations which may serve to enhance and/or distort knowledge

---

[7]Meissner (1992, p. 185) describes the tensions of interfacing psychoanalytic and religious thinking, each with its own discourse, reference points, and modes of conceptualization and symbolic connotation. He characterizes religious thinking as asserting "unequivocally that there is a God" and psychoanalytic thinking as being wholly concerned with the inner world of psychic experience. Such a characterization omits both religious thinking that questions who God is, and psychoanalytic thinking that interfaces external interpersonal and social realities with intrapsychic realities. Winnicott's concept of transitional phenomena, describing an area of illusion that is neither subjective nor objective, can be a useful bridging model between psychoanalytic and religious discourse (Meissner, 1992, p. 187).

of God.

Quantitative research on God representations has focussed on adjectives which people select to describe their conscious images of God. As a review of the literature will illustrate, when such adjectives are analyzed using factor analysis, they fall into groups which have been labelled by researchers to describe types of God representations (Spilka, Armatas, & Nussbaum, 1964; Gorsuch, 1968; Wootton, 1990). Four basic types of God representations are the loving God, the observing God, the absent God, and the wrathful God (Wootton, 1990). According to Spero's model of the formation of God representations (Spero, 1992, p. 141), what is studied in such quantitative research are projections of God representations. In this study, I will be using categories developed by Gorsuch (1968) and Wootton (1990) to describe the conscious types of God representations people may have.

Significance of the Problem

Defining the terms severity of traumatization and types of God representation in an introductory way allows us to elaborate the questions addressed in this study. Is there a significant relationship between the severity of childhood traumatization and conscious representations of God as loving, observing, absent and wrathful, such that the more severe the childhood traumatization, the less prevalent are women's loving and observing representations of God, and the more prevalent are their wrathful and absent representations of God?

When the literature on psychodynamic theories of traumatization is reviewed, one can appreciate the way in which traumatization impacts core structures of the personality. The more severe the traumatization, the greater the impact will be. A review of the literature on God representations highlights the theory that God representations are part of the structures of personality and its object representations. Given these two theories, one would deductively assume that traumatization affects and is affected by the structures of the personality, one of which is the God representation. This has been observed inductively by clinicians with clients experiencing post-traumatic stress disorder, especially those clients able to elaborate images of God (Mogenson, 1989; Bowman, 1989).

In a study of the inter-relationship between experiences of violence and assumptions about themselves, the world and others, Janoff Bulman (1989a) found that victims were more likely than nonvictims to view themselves less positively, see the world as random, and see interpersonal relationships as less benevolent and more malevolent. One could infer from these findings that God would be experienced as less benevolent and more malevolent. In contradiction to such findings, a study of Holocaust survivors demonstrated that Holocaust survivors and children of Holocaust survivors described themselves as religious more often than a control group (Carmil & Breznitz, 1991).

In a study of abused and nonabused elementary school children, the dimensions of wrathfulness, kindness and distance of God and parent concepts were compared (Johnson & Eastburg, 1992). There were no differences in the God concepts of abused and nonabused children, while abused children described parents as less kind and more wrathful than nonabused children. These findings raise questions about whether there is an inter-relationship between abuse and God representations in childhood and also whether a negative inter-relationship is more likely to become conscious in adulthood and not childhood.

When one looks beyond psychodynamic literature on traumatization and God representations, one finds literature that supports the inter-relationship between childhood abuse and God representations. In surveys and interviews of women who experienced incest in childhood, such women describe themselves as alienated from the Judeo-Christian religious traditions of their childhood (Poling, 1992; Imbens & Jonker, 1992). The opposite response is seen in a study of the autobiographical literature of Protestant evangelicals who experienced physical abuse in childhood. Greven (1990) illustrates how often these individuals affirm both loving and wrathful representations of a God who uses fear and the threat of punishment to obtain obedience. One could speculate that culture and gender may be crucial factors in whether adults embrace a God who resembles the abuser or rejects such a God. Indeed, the contradictions among the literature on abuse and religion may simply illustrate the need for research where factors of age, culture and gender are monitored. As well, such research may need to take into account subtle distinctions between God representations, religiosity, and assumptions about one's self, the world and interpersonal relationships.

While it is seemingly self evident that God representations and traumatization would be inter-related, this hypothesis has been explored by few theorists or clinicians. When such a hypothesis has been explored, findings are contradictory. The complexities of quantitatively or qualitatively exploring the inter-relationship between traumatization and God representations have not always been fully addressed. The theoretical writings of Mogenson (1989) and Fairbairn (1952) and the research of Justice (1984), Coons (1980), Higdon and Faheem (1984), Bowman, Coons, Jones and Oldstrom (1987), Bowman (1989), and Johnson and Eastburg (1992) make up the small body of literature dealing with the inter-relationship of traumatization and God representations.

In this study I will address the methodological complexities of research on intrapsychic phenomenon such as traumatization and God representations. The complexities are twofold. First, traumatization and God representations are conscious and unconscious. The more disturbing aspects of each are likely to be repressed, and those who have been traumatized as children may not have any conscious memories of such experiences. A self report on severity of traumatization may be limited by the changes in personality[8] and memory that can occur after trauma. Secondly, traumatization and God representations are inter-related bi-directionally, such that one's God representations may shape how one experiences traumatic stressors (that is, God representations may be considered part of the pre-existing personality structure, which, as van der Kolk (1987) has noted, may compound or alleviate the impact of traumatic stressors) and one's experience of traumatization may shape one's God representations.

As a first step in exploring this complex area of research, I will quantitatively explore the relationship between women's consciously remembered traumatization and conscious God representations. In discussing the results of this research, I will take into account the possibility of the repression of traumatic memories and disturbing God representations, and the bi-directional relationship between traumatization and God representations.

Besides addressing the complexity of research on God representations, traumatization and their inter-relationship, this study contributes to our knowledge of what shapes peoples' God representations. A case study approach has been used to describe individuals' God representations and to speculate on how these were formed (Rizzuto, 1979; McDargh, 1983; Spero, 1992). Meissner (1984) has elaborated a theory of how God representations are formed as people move through early childhood development. This study focuses on the way the critical event of traumatization may shape peoples' God representations.

This study also contributes to research on the impact of trauma at a psychodynamic level. Conclusions about the relationship between traumatization and God representations add to the literature on the relationship between traumatization and object relations (Fairbairn, 1952; Lindy, 1986; Blum, 1987; Krystal, 1988; Ulman & Brothers, 1988; McCann & Pearlman, 1990) and as such explores the impact that traumatization can have at the core of the personality. A current review of the psychoanalytic literature of child sexual abuse found only two empirical studies among the 48 articles reviewed (Wolf & Alpert, 1991).[9] The present study demonstrates a way of interfacing empirical findings with a psychodynamic model of traumatization and God representations.

---

[8]Titchener (1986) and Herman (1992) describe such changes, respectively, as post-traumatic decline and complex post-traumatic stress disorder.

[9]Wolf and Alpert did not include the many empirical studies of traumatization that assume a psychodynamic model of personality.

This research is clinically significant for pastoral clinicians who work with those who are traumatized, especially those who develop rigid faith systems out of their experiences of traumatization. The proposed model of the inter-relationship between traumatization and God representations and the quantitative research findings are intended to enhance our understanding of how we can work with this inter-relationship to facilitate healing.

The ultimate purpose of such research is to enhance our empathic response to those who experience traumatization. Towards that end, this research is intended ultimately for the community of faith, whose response to traumatization can have a great impact on either alleviating or compounding the most destructive effects of traumatic stressors.

CHAPTER TWO

REVIEW OF THE LITERATURE

Psychodynamic Theories of Traumatization

In the past two decades, there has been a growing appreciation for the profound impact of traumatic stressors at all levels of being: a neurological level, an intrapsychic level, the level of interpersonal relationships, a cultural level, and a faith/visional level.[1] This study will focus on the impact of traumatic stressors at an intrapsychic level. A psychodynamic model of personality will create a theoretical frame for understanding the inter-relationship between traumatization and God representations.

A basic assumption of any psychodynamic understanding of traumatization is that traumatic stressors have their most profound impact at the core level of personality. A review of structural/drive theory, self psychology, and object relations theory illustrates how definitions of the core level of personality shape theories on the impact of traumatic stressors.

Structural/Drive Theory

A structural model of personality is based upon Freudian and ego psychology, in which personality is described in terms of the psycho-economics of drives or instincts generated within the structures of ego, id and superego. Traumatization is understood primarily in terms of the ego and id. The impact

---

[1]Browning (1991) uses the word, visional, to describe the profound faith metaphors embedded in individual and community narratives. Both Poling (1992) and Graham (1992) have articulated practical theologies that describe this faith/visional level of family violence.

of traumatic stressors is threefold (Palombo, 1981). **First**, the traumatic stressor creates intense stimuli which flood the intrapsychic structures. The sympathetic nervous system is aroused, attention becomes concentrated on the immediate danger represented by the external stressors. These responses to the traumatic stressors prepare people to fight or flee for their lives.

When escape or fighting back is not possible, then intense stimuli quickly overwhelm the ego's ability to process it.[2] Freud (1926, p. 166) described this process metaphorically as the breaching of the stimulus barrier, the barrier which acts as a filter, allowing in as much stimuli as can be processed by the ego. When this barrier is breached, the ego is flooded with stimuli, and there is a subjective feeling of helplessness.

When children are exposed to traumatic stressors, it is the parents' role to act as a stimulus barrier:

> Normally the mother acts as a supplementary stimulus barrier for her infant. In abusive situations, the mother not only fails to supplement the child's stimulus barrier but contributes to---or allows another to contribute to---the trauma. (Tuohy, 1987, p. 29)

The term "cumulative trauma" describes the long-term interference with the abused child's development caused by the caretaker's failure to provide a protective shield from overwhelming stimuli (Khan, 1963).

The **second** effect of the traumatic stressor is that the stressor provokes unconscious material to break through into consciousness. Thus, just as the stimulus barrier is breached, so the repression barrier, which limits how much unconscious material filters through into consciousness, can also be breached when an individual experiences a traumatic stressor. Primary processes, drive derivatives and wishes which are usually repressed may fuse with stimuli provoked by the traumatic stressor.

---

[2]As Stolorow and Atwood (1992, p. 52) point out, the emphasis on "quantities of instinctual excitation overloading the capacities of an energy processing apparatus" assumes the myth of the isolated mind. They assert that "the essence of trauma lies in the experience of unbearable affect" which has not been regulated within the child-caregiver system (Stolorow & Atwood, 1992, p. 52).

The specific content of the repressed material may be related directly to the nature and meaning of the triggering traumatic event, or it may relate to dominant developmental issues and unresolved conflicts. (Palombo, 1981, p. 15)

The **third** effect of the traumatic stressor, which happens simultaneously with the bombardment of the ego, is that selected ego functions related to anxiety and the signaling of danger break down. The signal function of anxiety is not able to forewarn the ego of danger, because the traumatic stressor is outside of the ego's range of experience. The ego is not able to use defenses to cope with overwhelming stimuli and the breaking through of unconscious material. Secondary processes may temporarily cease to operate, and the ego is not able to integrate the flood of material the results from the traumatic stressor. The ego may have difficulty distinguishing between reality and fantasy, and memory may intertwine events and fantasies, as "the perception of the event becomes confused and colored by the inner upheaval" (Palombo, 1981, p. 16).

The multi-layered meaning of the event is shaped by the unconscious material released as the individual experiences the traumatic stressor, and later, as further unconscious material may be released during re-experiences of the traumatic stressor.

Trauma acts as an organizer around which unresolved conflicts, uncompleted developmental tasks and cognitive understanding coalesce into a psychic structure. (Palombo, 1981, p. 16)

Such "traumatic material" may remain "frozen" or "undigested" because of the ego's incapacity to process it.

The "frozen" or "undigested" quality of traumatic material is most clearly seen in nightmares and Rorschach responses of people with post-traumatic stress disorder (van der Kolk, Blitz, Burr, Sherry & Hartmann, 1984; van der Kolk & Ducey, 1989). The dreams are "an "undigested," concrete reliving of traumatic events, unmodified by the passage of time and unintegrated with other experiences" (van der Kolk & Ducey, 1989, p. 260). In these studies of nightmares and Rorschach responses, it was found that even those who denied preoccupation with trauma in their daily lives showed the unconscious mass of "frozen" material in the dreams and in their Rorschach responses.

[These Rorschach responses] confirm the clinical impression that people with severe PTSD are incapable of modulated affective experience; they either respond to affective stimuli with an intensity which is appropriate only to the traumatic situation, or they barely react at all. These Rorschach demonstrate the immediacy and concreteness of their experience, and the apparent lack of capacity to symbolize, fantasize or sublimate. (van der Kolk & Ducey, 1989, p. 267)

The "compulsion to repeat" first described by Freud (1914a) is an "attempt to symbolize the mute, concrete, unsymbolized experience" (van der Kolk & Ducey, 1989, p. 271). Treatment takes the form of "integrating the alien" (van der Kolk & Ducey, 1989, p. 271).[3]

In understanding the effect of traumatization on the core structure of the personality, one can visualize the frozen mass of traumatic material as channelling affective energy into "loops" that replay traumatic material. It is interesting that the Freudian metaphor of the economics of energy resonates with the physiological response to traumatic stressors: specifically, the symptoms of catecholamine depletion and autonomic hyperarousal.[4] Research suggests that the greater the degree of physiological arousal upon exposure to traumatic stressors, the greater will be the traumatization.

When traumatic stressors are repeated over a prolonged period, there are more enduring changes to the personality. Examples of such changes are evident in people who are held hostage under violent conditions like prisoner of war camps, concentration camps, and families in which physical, sexual and emotional violence are repeated over and over again. A new diagnostic category, complex post-traumatic stress disorder, has been proposed to describe the alterations in affect regulation, consciousness, self perception, perception of the perpetrator, relations with others and systems of meaning seen among people subjected to totalitarian control over a prolonged period (Herman, 1992, pp. 118-122).

Poling (1991, pp. 102-109) has summarized the long term effects of repeated sexual abuse on the structures and drives of the personality.[5] Ego functioning is impaired, particularly the capacity for reality testing. The capacity of the superego to set realistic goals and limits may be impaired. Libidinal energies may

---

[3]Wilmer (1986), in research on combat nightmares, found that in the process of therapy, combat dreams shifted from being recurring replicas of combat experience, to dreams with elements from traumatic experiences intermingled with experiences from everyday life. Wilmer suggested that such dreams demonstrate the increasing capacity to symbolize that is part of the healing of trauma.

[4]"Physiological changes [following trauma] can, in fact, account for most post-traumatic symptomatology: (1) the tendency to react to relatively minor stimuli as if it were a recurrence of the trauma...; (2) visual and motoric reliving experiences ...; (3) persistent hyperarousal...; (4) compulsive re-exposure to circumstances reminiscent of the trauma" (van der Kolk, 1988, p. 275).

[5]For an excellent overview of the psychoanalytic literature on sexual abuse, see Wolf and Albert (1991). As these authors note, the psychodynamic literature on child sexual abuse is mostly reported in case studies (only two of the 48 articles reviewed were empirical studies).

be misdirected into symbiotic relationships or isolation, particularly when core issues are pregenital, and not oedipal or phallic. Aggression may take the form of rage or helplessness. Instead of a healthy narcissism that functions both to affirm and critique the self, there may be an alternation between grandiosity and self devaluation. Poling also highlights the role of gender differences: women tend toward symbiotic relationships, helplessness and self devaluation, while men tend toward isolation, rage and grandiosity.

Self Psychology

In Kohut's self psychological model, the self is added to the structural model of ego, id, and superego, and is understood as a supraordinate structure of personality. In self psychology, the focus is not on the psycho-economics of drives and the development of ego functions, but on the development of the psychic structure of the self. The self is understood as a supraordinate structure of the personality that develops as the child is able to mature in an empathic environment.

Kohut described the internal representations of empathic caretakers as selfobjects, which are experienced by the developing child as part of him or herself. When the child is exposed to traumatic stressors, the empathic parent will provide the psychological structures to deal with anxiety (Kohut, 1971 pp. 235-237). The child experiences the parent's merger as if the parent were part of him or herself.

An important aspect of Kohut's theory is his understanding of our need for selfobjects throughout the transitions and crises not only of infancy and childhood, but adulthood (Kohut, 1984, p. 199). Even as Kohut saw the ability to use selfobjects throughout life as crucial to health and maturity, so too did he see the failure of selfobjects as the cause of human pain:

> The fear of death and the fear of psychoses are, in many instances, the expression of the fear of loss of the empathetic milieu that in responding to the self keeps it psychologically alive. (Kohut, 1982, p. 397)

Kohut's theory on the crucial role of the empathic milieu elaborates the role of the environment in creating stability for the self when it is threatened during psychic traumatization. If there is an empathic milieu, individuals who experience the disintegration of self during psychic traumatization can temporarily borrow the psychological structures of those in the empathic milieu, much as an infant experiencing anxiety merges with the psychological structures of the caregiver, until such structures can become internalized:

If empathetic caregivers recognize the manifestations of the fragmentation and respond appropriately with a dose of mirroring or allowing themselves to become the target for idealization, the fragmentation experience will be short lived. (Muslin, 1985, p. 213)

Two specific "selfobject functions," the mirroring selfobject function and the idealized parent imago, are important for coping with traumatization, especially during childhood. The mirroring selfobject function is created as the parent responds to and confirms the child's "innate sense of vigor, greatness and perfection" (Kohut & Wolf, 1978, p. 414). Traumatized children may be robbed of their sense of potency and power. A responsive caretaker can, through mirroring, reinstate the child's sense of vigor and power, which the child can gradually internalize.

The second selfobject function crucial for development of the self is the idealized parent imago, "an image of calmness, infallibility and omnipotence" (Kohut & Wolf, 1978, p. 414). Such a selfobject function is crucial for a traumatized child, or indeed adult, who needs to re-experience the world as safe, and who may have a distorted perception of their vulnerability and the danger of recurrent traumatization.

Traumatization is compounded when parents are not able to fulfill these functions, and is most severe when the caretaker is the abuser. In therapy, children abused by a caretaker show an "enormous object hunger," over-idealizing the therapist (Green, 1978, p. 95; Cornett, 1985, p. 84). The child who is not be able to internalize strengthening and soothing functions, especially in relation to the traumatization, will be psychologically unable to cope with further traumatization.

Another way to understand the central effect of traumatic stressors is that they shatter the "archaic narcissistic fantasies central to the organization of self-experience" (Ulman & Brothers, 1988, p. xii). Attempts to restore these fantasies shape the unconscious meaning of the traumatic event. The severe disruption of selfobject relations caused by traumatization may specifically involve a split between the omnipotent, grandiose self, or the conscious invulnerable self, and the hidden victim self introject, or the unconscious vulnerable self (Brende, 1983; Hymer, 1984).

In self psychology, psychic traumatization threatens the core of the personality, the self, since it has the potential of fragmenting the self.[6] The

---

[6]Stolorow and Atwood (1992) see the essence of trauma as a failure of the child-caregiver system, whose responsibility it is to regulate affect.

profound impact of traumatic stressors on the individual is usually attributed to the life-threatening qualities of the stressor (for example, the life-threatening quality of combat, a natural disaster, or a sexual or physical assault). From a self psychological perspective, the ultimate threat to being is not to one's physical life, but to one's self (Kohut, 1985, p. 264). Traumatization is understood as the experiencing and re-experiencing of the threat to the self, and the momentary or extended disintegration of the self that may occur (Brende, 1983; Brende & Parson, 1985; Parson, 1988; Ulman & Brothers, 1988).

Evidence for traumatization as a threat to the self may be inferred from the nature of repetitive dreams replaying traumatic material. Such dreams are described by Kohut as self-state dreams which, unlike everyday dreams, describe danger to the self (Kohut, 1977; Tolpin, 1983).

Object Relations Theory

The term, object relations theory, refers to those theorists in the psychodynamic tradition who understand drives or instincts as object-seeking rather than pleasure-seeking. With this perspective, healthy psychological development is determined by the quality of the ego's relationship to internal objects, which shape the way individuals relate to people (external objects). From an object relations perspective, traumatization shapes the quality of the ego's relationship to internal objects:

> What are primarily repressed are neither intolerably guilty impulses nor intolerably unpleasant memories, but intolerably bad internalized objects... The victim of sexual assault resists the revival of the traumatic memory primarily because this memory represents a record of a relationship with a bad object" (Fairbairn, 1952, p. 62 & 63).

In the process of traumatization and repression, the child elaborates the traumatic memory, intermingling fact and fantasy to create a psychic reality. Describing the external reality as "fact," however, may imply a "pure outer reality out there, unchanging and the same for all" (Gediman, 1991, p. 388). A more accurate description of the inter-relationship between outer and inner reality may be a relational-intrapsychic model which acknowledges both the interpersonal experience of abuse (the outer/relational reality) and the internalizations of that experience (the intrapsychic reality).

> [The] interpersonal reality which is represented intrapsychically cannot be defined as a simple replica of objectively observable interactions between the patient and his or her primal object. It consists, rather, of imagos. (Gediman, 1991, p. 392)

The most profound effects of traumatization are the identifications formed with the internal objects which represent the external people involved in the trauma.   For example, in traumatization resulting from sexual assault, the assailant becomes internally represented. Others who may be involved during the traumatization---parents, friends, the police, personnel from social services, the hospital and the judicial system---also become internally represented.   While destructive identifications are formed with the internal representations of the aggressor or others who have a negative impact, creative identifications may also be formed with "the comforter, and with love objects in their caretaking and sustaining role" (Blum, 1987, p. 611). The variety of identifications that arise out of traumatization may be "adaptive or maladaptive, beneficial or pathogenic, transient or permanent" (Blum, 1987, p. 610).

Trauma may have a beneficial effect of "reinforcing a dominant developmental phase" when the child, or indeed adult, has powerful identifications with objects who maintained stability during the traumatization (Blum, 1987, p. 626). An example of this are the infants who stayed calm during the bombing of London in the second World War because they were in the presence of calm, reassuring parents (A. Freud & Burlingham, 1944).

The most striking identification formed out of traumatization is that with the aggressor (Ferenczi, 1932; A. Freud, 1936). There is an automatic identification with the aggressor in states of traumatic terror: "the helplessness of the ego is compensated for by the identification with the aggressor" (Blum, 1987, p. 613).[7]

Extensive psychological domination has a profound impact from an object relations perspective (Herman, 1992, pp. 74-95). At risk are the victim's "sense of self in relation to others" (Herman, 1992, p. 77) and "her internal images of connection to others" (Herman, 1992, p. 80).   Extension psychological domination destroys both external relationships and internal representations. This can happen in situations of captivity: in political prisons, violent marriage relationships and in cults. Not only are internal relationships with significant others threatened and at times destroyed, but the aggressor comes to dominate the inner world, long after external captivity ends:

> The sense that the perpetrator is still present, even after liberation, [is] a major alteration in the victim's relational world. (Herman, 1992, p. 91)

---

[7]Experiences of sexual abuse involving manipulation of affection and misrepresentation of social standards around sexual behavior may not provoke the feelings of powerlessness and danger central to traumatization (Kendall-Tackett, Meyer Williams & Finkelhor, 1993, p. 174). Internal representations of such aggressors will be more associated with traumatic sexualization and less with powerlessness.

Another way to understand traumatization from an object relations perspective is in terms of the difference between identifications with "good" and "bad" objects during traumatization. Adaptive and beneficial identifications facilitate a healthy transition through the crisis of traumatization, and become incorporated[8] into the ego. This type of internalization is one which builds up psychic structures (Guntrip, 1969). This can be likened to the way food is digested and becomes "assimilated by the organism and serves as aliment for the building and energizing of bodily structure and processes" (Eagle, 1983, p. 78). The maladaptive and pathogenic identifications are internalized in a different way:

> In bad experiences, the bad object is internalized as object, undigested and unassimilated, and hence remains as a foreign body within the psychic structure of the individual. (Eagle, 1983, p. 78)

The metaphor of traumatic material or object identifications remaining undigested is useful from a structural or object relations perspective. The "undigested" identifications with bad objects that may result from traumatization can be seen in dreams or responses to Rorschach ink blots. As well, they may be acted out unconsciously and uncovered in the process of therapy.

While some object relations theorists have focused on the psychodynamics between internal objects that coalesce in traumatization, others have used an object relations perspective in conjunction with a Piagetian understanding of cognitive development, to describe the schemata of self and the world that are disrupted during traumatization (Lifton, 1976, 1979, 1988; Janoff-Bulman, 1985, 1989a, 1989b, 1992; McCann & Pearlman, 1990). The internal representations of self, others, and God can be understood as the underlying metaphors that give rise to the larger schemata of self and the world, which become the conceptual frameworks for organizing and interpreting experience. Both of these levels, 1) the deep underlying metaphors of self, others and God, and 2) the complex cognitive representations of self, others and God, may operate at an unconscious or preconscious level of awareness.

In the normal transitions and crises of development, schemata change through the processes of accommodation and assimilation (Piaget, 1971). During traumatization, the external events and internal responses may shatter the complex cognitive schemata that are used to make sense of what is happening. Individuals may be unable to accommodate the experience of traumatic stressors and traumatization because they so profoundly disrupt cognitive schemata concerning

---

[8]Eagle (1983, p. 79) notes the confusion in the literature around the terms, identification, introjection and incorporation. He suggests that "what Fairbairn wants to convey by internalized object and what others want to convey by the concept of introjection is the idea that what is taken in is not fully integrated into one's self and organization."

existential beliefs.

> The experience does not fit into existing conceptual schemata: it
> overwhelms. This precludes accommodation and assimilation of the
> experience; leaving the experience to be organized on a sensorimotor or
> iconic level---as horrific images, visceral sensations, or as
> fight/flight/freeze reactions. (van der Kolk, 1988, p. 282)

This cognitive model resonates with a psychodynamic metaphor of traumatic
material as "frozen" or "undigested" and suggests that one reason such material
remains frozen is because it is organized on a sensorimotor or iconic level.

Not only do traumatic stressors disrupt the processes of accommodation and
assimilation; they may cause ongoing difficulties with these cognitive processes.
In a study comparing children who had been severely abused with children who
had not experienced abuse, Fish-Murray, Koby and van der Kolk (1987, p. 101)
stated

> Thus far, our strongest finding in these abused children has been the
> inflexibility of organized schemata and structures in all domains.

Cognitive schemata that may be disrupted and become inflexible during and after
traumatization may concern existential cognitive schemata (what Lifton (1988)
calls the disruption of life symbols) and schemata related to moral reasoning. As
Fish-Murray, Koby and van der Kolk (1987, p. 99) describe

> The standards of the abused children were very different from the controls;
> for example, they did not have the same concepts of justice and
> responsibility for rules. They tended to think that rules were made by the
> largest male in the place, and physical punishment was the reason for not
> breaking them.

Janoff-Bulman (1985) describes three adult assumptions about the self and the
world that are shattered during trauma: the belief in personal invulnerability, the
perception of the world as positive, and the perception of the self as positive.
Victims are more likely to see the self as unworthy, interpersonal relations as
malevolent, and the world as random (Janoff-Bulman, 1989a).

> [Traumatic events] shatter the construction of the self that is formed and
> sustained in relation to others. They undermine the belief systems that
> give meaning to human experience. They violate the victim's faith in a
> natural or divine order and cast the victim into a state of existential crisis.
> (Herman, 1992, p. 51)

One may conclude that in all psychodynamic theories, traumatization is thought to have its most profound impact at the core level of the personality: in structural theory, the psycho-economics of energy generated by instincts; in self psychology, the cohesion of the self; in object relations theory, the object representations at the core of the personality. This impact may be acute, and seen most clearly in the alternation between intrusion of traumatic memories and constriction of affect. When traumatic stressors are repeated and prolonged, within the context of overpowering relationships, then the impact of traumatization will not simply be acute, but will cause alterations in affect regulation, consciousness, internal representations, relationships and systems of meaning.

A second area of agreement among the three models is that in traumatization, powerful internal meanings and figures coalesce. According to structural theory, the images, sensations, and feelings associated with the traumatic stressors become merged with powerful unconscious images, thoughts and feelings released through traumatization. From a self psychological perspective, archaic narcissistic fantasies central to the organization of self-experience are disrupted, and splits occur between the omnipotent, grandiose self (the conscious invulnerable self) and the hidden victim self introject (the unconscious vulnerable self). According to object relations theory, the process of traumatization causes powerful internal figures associated with aspects of the trauma to coalesce. All psychodynamic theories agree that powerful internal dramas, myths, images, and associations converge in the process of traumatization.

A third area of agreement is that the powerful, internal response to traumatic stressors is so overwhelming that it is largely repressed, in as much as it can be. The alternation between intrusion and avoidance of images, feelings, sensations, and thoughts associated with the traumatization is the hallmark of post-traumatic stress (Horowitz, 1976). From a psychodynamic perspective, these images, feelings, sensations and thoughts associated with traumatization which alternately intrude and are avoided are the psychodynamic configurations that formed during traumatization (for example, the shattered fantasies of safety and power, or the internal representations). In simple post-traumatic stress disorder, the alternation between intrusion and constriction may create opportunities for working through psychodynamic configurations associated with traumatization. In complex post-traumatic stress disorder, psychodynamic configurations associated with traumatization will cause profound alterations in consciousness, affect regulation, internal representations, relationships and systems of meaning.

Empirical Measures of Psychic Traumatization

The most widely used measure of traumatization is the Impact of Event Scale, developed by Horowitz, Wilner and Alvarez (1979). Its purpose is to measure the stress associated with traumatic events, in terms of 1) intrusive experiences, such as ideas, feelings or nightmares and 2) avoidance of ideas, feelings and situations associated with the traumatic event.

Unfortunately, the Impact of Event Scale yields limited information on severity of traumatization. It can be used to measure the first factor which van der Kolk (1987) describes, the severity of traumatic stressors, but is only useful when people are in the acute stage of traumatization, that is, when the trauma has just occurred or is just being re-experienced.

There have been several recent studies utilizing Rorschach cards to diagnose post-traumatic stress disorder (Salley & Teiling, 1984; Carr, 1984; Kowitt, 1985; van der Kolk & Ducey, 1989). Of these, van der Kolk and Ducey's study is the most comprehensive. They found that Rorschach responses of combat veterans with PTSD showed an unmodified reliving of traumatic material, even among those who did not consciously experience the intrusion of traumatic material. Van der Kolk and Ducey demonstrate the usefulness of using the Rorschach Inkblot Test to diagnose post-traumatic stress disorder, especially in those who use avoidance as a defence against the intrusiveness of traumatic material.

For the purposes of studying severity of traumatization, utilizing Rorschach cards may have the advantage of bypassing conscious defenses and revealing the presence of traumatic material. The disadvantages of using Rorschach cards is that, first, they have not been tested with stressors other than combat. It may be that responses are less clearly associated with traumatic stressors such as early sexual or physical child abuse and may be more subject to interpretation. A second disadvantage is that the time-consuming nature of the test would make sample size limited, unless particular cards were used, for example, the five chromatic cards (II, III, VIII, IX, X) which, in Van der Kolk and Ducey's study "provoked uncontrolled and apparently trauma-related responses" (van der Kolk & Ducey, 1989, p. 263). In terms of measuring severity of traumatization, these cards could be used to determine whether traumatic stressors were severe enough to have lasting consequences and a profound, chronic psychodynamic impact. Unfortunately, the use of Rorschach cards in evaluating PTSD is limited to this one study of combat veterans, and the validity of such a measure would have to be demonstrated first with other severe traumatic stressors.

The only measure for severity of traumatization, and one which utilizes van der Kolk's factors, is an extensive questionnaire developed by Herman & van der

Kolk, called the Traumatic Antecedents Questionnaire (Herman & van der Kolk, 1990). The questionnaire, used in an interview format, has 100 questions. In Parts One and Two information is gathered on religion and social support, current health of the interviewee, including alcohol consumption, smoking, use of prescriptive and non prescriptive drugs, major illnesses, self-injurious behaviors, hospitalizations and pregnancies. Part Three surveys family of origin demographics, including information on who in the family was affectionate, treated the interviewee as special, or with whom the interviewee felt safe. Part Four focuses on childhood caretakers and separations; Part Five on peer relationships and childhood strengths; Part Six on family alcoholism. In Part Seven, on family discipline and conflict resolution, questions move from asking about punishment to the use of violence in conflict resolution. The 10 questions on violence are structured to yield extensive descriptions of incidents of violence and the effect it had on the interviewee. In Part Eight, on early sexual experiences, questions move from family attitudes towards sex to childhood and adolescent sexual experiences. As in the preceding section, the 14 questions on sexual abuse elicit extensive information on the nature, frequency and impact of the abuse. The last section, Part Nine, asks interviewees to name the most serious of the traumatic experiences discussed. The closing three questions concern the interviewees' most helpful means of coping, and what advice they would give to others on the basis of their experiences.

The questionnaire is well constructed, in that it is designed to elicit full descriptions of traumatic sexual and physical abuse and witnessing domestic violence, and is structured in a way that gently leads interviewees into more and more vulnerable areas. It is detailed enough to ensure that questioning among participants is consistent and can yield specific information on different aspects of traumatization, such as social support, evidence of a psychiatric history or alcohol abuse, severity of traumatic stressor, and developmental stage at which abuse occurred. In the third chapter, I will describe how this questionnaire has been used to yield quantitative data on severity of traumatization.

The Nature of Representations

Freud (1914b) was the first to describe object representations formed in the first six years, which he called imagos or prototypes[9] for later relationships. Such representations are evoked in the transference and may be tied to particular prototypes: father-imago, mother-imago, brother-imago (Freud, 1912). Freud understood these imagos as being the internal objects of wishes energized by the instincts of libido and aggression.

Representations can also be understood from a cognitive developmental perspective as the ability of a child to internally represent any kind of external experience, not simply the experience of significant people in a child's life (Piaget, 1945). The capacity to internally represent what is external is a crucial transition in the overall development of the child. As was noted earlier, these first internal representations may be thought of as the deep structure for the more complex representations of self, others and God which develop.

Some theorists (Schafer, 1968, 1976) describe object representations simply as ideas, thoughts and information that help to create meaning. Others (Stierlin, 1970) ascribe functions to object representations, similar to ego functions. Rizzuto (1979) highlights the debate between these two positions and articulates the implicit viewpoint of many object relations theorists, that object representations are

> ...A sort of mental entity, organization, structure, content, schema or engram...capable of having psychic effects: it persecutes, provokes anxiety (and therefore splitting), consoles, sustains, forms mental structures, is "located" in the ego, and so on. (Rizzuto, 1979, p. 74)

Rizzuto's own position is that object representations are instances of the larger processes of representing, remembering, fantasizing, interpreting and integrating experiences. Compounded memories become synthesized as object representations (Rizzuto, 1979, p. 77). Her position contrasts with the implications of many object relations theorists that object representations are discrete, isolated from memory process, and entities with lives of their own.

---

[9]The early use of multiple terms, such as imago and prototype when referring to representations may have contributed to what Wootton (1990, pp. 40-41) describes as the confusion in the literature on God representations between the terms imago, image, concept, and representation. Spero (1992, p. 134) uses the terms, object image to describe "an unorganized, unstructured, whole or part perception"; object representation to describe "a more organized, structured, and internalized image"; and object concept to describe "a larger consolidation of many related object representations."

Recent theoretical models of representations reflect Rizzuto's understanding of object representations in that they draw together an object relations model with a Piagetian model of complex cognitive schemata that are formed through developmental transitions and crises (Lifton, 1976, 1979, 1988; Janoff-Bulman, 1985, 1989a, 1989b; McCann & Pearlman, 1990). In this model, object representations can be understood as the deep structure which gives rise to complex cognitive schemata of self, others and God.

These theorists highlight how some of these schemata may describe existential beliefs, which become the broadest frameworks for organizing experience. These provide frames of reference for the world as just, predictable and controllable. Implicit or explicit in these would be one's operational belief system. These schemata help one understand why events happen (causality), describe one's orientation to the future (hope/despair), describe the power dynamics between self and others, self and the world, and self and God (also described as locus of control) (McCann & Pearlman, 1990, pp. 62-66).

Empirical Studies on Representations

Empirical Measures of Representations

Empirical measures of representations have been developed by psychometrists to assess people's object relations along a developmental continuum. Mayman and his colleagues have developed several instruments for assessing object representations. In the Early Memories Test (Mayman, 1968), individuals describe their early memories. The concept validity of this test rests on three suppositions: first, that early memories describe fantasies that illustrate underlying structures of the personality; second, that early memories reveal images of the self in relation to others; third, that early memories reveal underlying themes about peoples' representational worlds, which can be used to describe their object relations.

Similar theoretical suppositions are used by Krohn and Mayman (1974) in their Object Representation Scale for Dreams. Krohn and Mayman (1974) found that there were high correlations between ratings of object relations, as measured by Rorschach cards, the Early Memories Test and the Object Representation Scale for Dreams. With both the Early Memories Test and the Object Representation Scale for Dreams, there is an assumption that one's object relations are the deep structure that generates the texts of dreams and early memories. Since both dreams and early memories presumably access the unconscious to a greater degree than other autobiographical texts, there is more likelihood of accessing this deep, unconscious level of the personality. A systematic thematic analysis of the texts of dreams and early memories can be used to assess developmental levels of object relations.

Urist (1977) used responses to Rorschach cards to develop a seven point scale for assessing the individual's capacity to experience self and others as mutually autonomous within relationships. Stages on the seven point scale describe the interaction between figures seen on each card. At one end of the scale are descriptions of figures who are separate, autonomous and engaged in reciprocal, mutual interactions. At the other end of the scale are descriptions of figures who were "swallowed up, devoured, or generally overwhelmed by forces completely beyond their control" (Urist, 1977, p. 5). Urist's description of the fifth range on the scale is of special interest in terms of assessing trauma and/or God representations:

> The nature of the relationship between figures is characterized by a theme of malevolent control of one figure by another. Themes of influencing, controlling, casting spells are present. One figure may literally or figuratively be in the clutches of another... On the one hand, figures may be seen as powerful and helpless, while at the same time others are omnipotent and controlling. (Urist, 1977, p. 5)

The scale has the potential to be used for inferring the relationship between self representations and God representations. The great advantage of such a scale is that God representations are not assessed in isolation, but in terms of the inter-relationship between self and God representations. A disadvantage, for the purposes of this study, is the time-consuming nature of administering Rorschach cards and the pioneer use of Urist's scale for this purpose.

Urist found that ratings of mutuality of autonomy in Rorschach imagery was highly inter-correlated with similar ratings done with autobiographical accounts and ratings by staff of patients' relational behavior. The study demonstrates "the structural argument that individuals tend to experience self-other relationships in consistent, enduring characteristic ways that can be defined for each individual along a developmental continuum" (Urist, 1977, p. 3).

Blatt, Brenneis, Schimek and Glick (1976) developed a comprehensive scale for assessing an individual's representational world through Rorschach card responses. They assume that "any image attributed to an essentially ambiguous stimulus must be shaped by the organizing characteristics of the representational world" (Blatt & Lerner, 1983, p. 9). As in studies by Urist and Mayman and his colleagues, Blatt and his colleagues develop a detailed scale for assessing the content and the structure of object representations as an enduring dimension of personality. Blatt and Lerner (1983) in reviewing the literature on the use of Rorschach figures for assessing individuals' representational worlds conclude:

In summary, Rorschach responses with human content appear to be vivid expressions of important interpersonal relationships and transactions which are internalized by the individual as cognitive structures which continually influence, shape and color the experiences of subsequent situations and relationships. (Blatt & Lerner, 1983)

A measure of object relations which does not use Rorschach cards has been developed by Bell and his colleagues. Bell (1988) developed a true-false self report with items describing characteristic patterns of relationships. The Bell Object Relations and Reality Testing Inventory is designed to measure four factors of object relations: alienation, insecure attachment, egocentricity, and social incompetence (Billington & Bell, 1985; Bell, 1988). Bell has demonstrated that this inventory is more reliable and valid than projective measures (Bell et al., 1986; Bell, 1988). Replication studies attest to its internal consistency and show considerable factorial invariance (Bell, 1988).

There have been recent models which integrate object relations theory and cognitive development. One instrument designed from this theoretical perspective measures changes in cognitive schemata about self, others and the world. The World Assumptions Scale, designed by Janoff-Bulman (1989a) is a series of assumptions which describe how people view themselves, others and the world. Janoff-Bulman used the instrument with a sample of traumatized and non-traumatized individuals. This instrument, used in conjunction with empirical instruments measuring object relations, may be a means of demonstrating the theoretical inter-relationship between object relations and cognitive schemata.

The empirical measures of object relations described above provide a means of assessing object relations in terms of a developmental continuum and diagnostic categories. These measures do not focus on particular representations, such as representations of mother, father, or God. However, they could be used to infer how such figures would be represented (as I speculated earlier, with Urist's scale). Janoff-Bulman's World Assumptions Scale may be used to infer both schemata about God, self and others, and underlying metaphors of God, self and others. Use of such scales might be a means for future research on how the unconscious dimension of God and self representations can be assessed.

Object relations scales have not been used to assess how particular disruptive life events such as traumatic stressors shape object relations. When one considers that Rorschach cards evoke images specific to the traumatic stressor of combat (van der Kolk & Ducey, 1989), and that the representational world is revealed in Rorschach responses, then one might conclude that as a traumatic stressor, combat has the potential to disrupt the representational world in a profound and enduring way. This could be demonstrated through further studies utilizing Rorschach responses to study both post-traumatic stress and object representations.

The World Assumptions Scale has been used to empirically demonstrate the inter-relationship between trauma and schemata of self, others and the world. Janoff-Bulman (1989a) found that those who had been traumatized differed from those who hadn't in terms of viewing 1) themselves less positively, 2) interpersonal relationships as less benevolent, and 3) the world as random. One can infer from these findings that underlying metaphors of God and self, and schemata of existential beliefs are inter-related to traumatization.

In future areas of research, the combined use of object relations measures with measures of cognitive schemata could highlight the way traumatization affects God, self and other representations at various levels: the deep structural level of object relations, and the complex cognitive schemata of self, others and God.

Empirical Measures of God Representations

God representations measures can be categorized by the psychometric techniques used: 1) projective techniques, 2) semantic differential techniques, 3) The Q-sort technique and 4) factor analyses. I will review the research utilizing these categories, describing these measures in terms of their construction and use, and evaluating them in terms of their usefulness in research on traumatization and God representations.

Projective techniques

The first use of a projective technique to investigate God representations was done by Harms (1944). He asked children and adolescents to draw the Deity. In analyzing the thousands of pictures, he discerned three stages: a fairy tale stage, a realistic stage and an individualistic stage. Heller (1986) expanded this research, asking children to draw God, tell stories about God, play the role of God, and talk about God in a semi-structured interview. Sifting through his data, he developed a typology of God representations. This creative study, unfortunately, did not utilize multiple raters, nor did he consider the validity of his methodology.

A second early use of projective techniques to study images of God was the use of pictures to evoke peoples' images of God (Godin & Coupez, 1957). The pictures consisted of seven pictures that were not explicitly religious, and five that were. Participants were instructed to tell a story about each picture, and then were asked specific questions about the story when the spontaneous story-telling had finished. In their sample of 50 Roman Catholic girls, Godin and Coupez found that religious associations were low for the first seven pictures and high for the last five. They concluded that in order to study religious associations, it is important to have pictures that both have explicit religious content, and can offer "possibilities of purely secular associations in spite of the material presence of religious elements" (Godin & Coupez, 1957, p. 270). While the authors suggest many further areas of research, this projective technique is not developed further in the literature on projective techniques and God representations.

Rizzuto (1979) used the same technique as Harms (1944) and Heller (1986), of asking people to draw their God representation. She then interviewed them using a questionnaire she called the God Questionnaire. She reports in a narrative fashion on the people she interviewed. Her research is not qualitative, because she does not code answers and compare coded answers between participants, and it is not quantitative because she does not assign any numerical value to descriptions of God. Her study is best described as case studies of peoples' God representations.

Rorschach ink-blot cards were used by Eisenman, Bernard, and Hannon (1966). In their study, participants ranked Rorschach cards for their similarity to God and they completed two scales, benevolence and potency, based on the semantic differential technique. Larsen and Knapp (1969) made their own ink blots and had participants rate the ink blots on semantic scales according to how aptly they symbolized God. Since standardized instructions for Rorschach cards were not used, there was no means of scoring answers using Rorschach scoring procedures. In order to use the cards in the way they did, researchers would need to have a large norming group and make an attempt to standardize scoring procedures. It may be that a future area of research can utilize Rorschach cards to focus on a particular representation (that of God). With a large enough sample it may be possible to develop norming scales for God representations. This would yield rich descriptions of both the conscious and unconscious God representations. Unfortunately, such a scoring procedure was not available for this study on traumatization and God representations.

Most recently, Johnson and Eastburg (1992) developed a story completion projective test of God and parental representations for children ranging in age from five to thirteen years. The stories were about open-ended hypothetical situations where children described what action God or parents would take. The actions taken were categorized as portraying kindness/love, wrathfulness and distance. Two raters were used, with high inter-rater reliability. The authors arrived at these three dimensions of God and parental representations from a literature review of God representations measures. In their rating, they do not assume that the children's God representations will be uni-dimensional (that is, kind or wrathful or distant) but rather three dimensional (that is, kind and wrathful and distant). This allows for a multi-valent God and parental representation.

Johnson and Eastburg (1992) used their projective test with a sample of 60 children; half from a residential treatment program for children with experiences of physical and/or sexual abuse. They found no significant difference in the God representations of abused and non-abused children. Interestingly enough, God was often viewed as simultaneously kind, wrathful and distant. There was a significant difference in parental representations, with abused children rating parents as less kind and more wrathful than nonabused children. Unlike the God representations, the parental representations were not multidimensional; that is, in parental representations distance was not combined with either kindness or wrathfulness.

The authors discuss these findings in terms of Justice and Lambert's (1986) finding that adult patients who report histories of sexual abuse also report more negative God images than patients who do not report a history of sexual abuse. They conclude that "the effects of parental abuse on God concept may only appear later in development" and/or that "young children are more psychologically invested in denying the existence of abusive traits in the divine being" (Johnson & Eastburg, 1992, p. 240). They also speculate that the lack of correlation between God and parental concepts may indicate that these concepts develop independently, and/or are formed from different sources. The implications of their findings will be more fully explored in the concluding section of this chapter. Their research does demonstrate the potential of projective techniques in exploring God representations of children who have been abused, and illustrates how a measure that allows for a multi-dimensional God representation can yield intriguing findings.

Semantic differential technique

The semantic differential technique developed by Osgood, Suci and Tannenbaum (1957) is both an item format and also a theory of the meaning of concepts. The semantic differential technique as an item format rates a concept using a scale of bipolar adjectives. An example of such an item would be the following:

GOD: kind__:__:__:__:__:__:__cruel.

As a theory of meaning the semantic differential technique seeks to determine the general meaning of concepts, as measured by three dimensions: 1. evaluation (for example, good vs. bad; safe vs. dangerous), 2) potency (for example, strong vs. weak; firm vs. yielding) and 3) activity (for example, active vs. passive;

moving vs. still). Osgood, Suci and Tannenbaum developed 12 particular bipolar adjectival scales which they claimed measured all three dimensions: active-passive, friendly-unfriendly, good-bad, important-unimportant, large-small, meaningful-meaningless, near-far, personal-impersonal, pleasant-unpleasant, private-public, sharp-dull, strong-weak. Two of the concepts widely tested in evaluating the dimensions of meanings were God and prayer. Using the scale in the manner it was intended, one simply can measure to what extent God or prayer are viewed in terms of the evaluative, potent and active dimensions of meaning. There are many theoretical critiques of this theory of meaning, most of them concerning the limited construct of meaning. An obvious critique is that some adjectives seem nonsensical when used to describe concepts like God and prayer: for example, the bipolar adjectives, sharp versus dull.

Some of the research on God representations has utilized the particular scales developed by Osgood, Suci and Tannenbaum. For example, Heise (1965) used the semantic differential technique with a sample of naval enlistees to explore their concept of God. He found that this population tended to see God as high on the evaluation factor, moderate on the activity factor, and low on the potency factor. The weakness of using the scales as Heise did is that one must carefully review the validity of their construct of meaning. One must also consider the limitations of describing the richness and fullness of God imagery with simply 12 pairs of bipolar adjectives.

Others have used the bipolar adjectival scale to develop their own items. Tjart and Boersma (1978) used Osgood's semantic differential items of God and prayer to assess the religious values of a group of eighth graders, half in public schools and half in Christian schools. They were investigating whether Christian schools inculcate values more effectively than public schools. The same criticisms made of Heise's study pertain to this study.

Benson and Spilka (1973) developed a 13 item semantic differential scale to measure loving and controlling God images, which they used in conjunction with a 64 adjective Q-sort developed by Spilka, Armatas and Nussbaum (1964), which will be described shortly. The Loving God Index was the score calculated from the following five pairs of adjectives: rejecting-accepting, loving-hating, damning-saving, unforgiving-forgiving, and approving-disapproving. Each item was scored from zero to six, with a maximum score of 30. The Controlling God Index was the score calculated from the following five pairs of adjectives: demanding-not demanding, freeing-restricting, controlling-uncontrolling, strict-lenient, and permissive-rigid. A sample of 50 Lutherans was used to measure scale homogeneity in order to demonstrate that each scale measured one homogenous dimension of God and not several dimensions.

A weakness of this index is its construction. The authors do not describe how they selected the adjectives they did. Construction would be sounder if adjectives were elicited from various sources, such as religious texts, or from a pool of adjectives gathered from a sample of people. The construct validity of the index presumes that these are two predominant dimensions of the God representation. The authors do not refer to the sources of this assumption. Finally, a difficulty with a bipolar item format is that participants have to choose either the positive or negative adjectives and cannot combine them (as in a loving and hating God) for a more richly ambivalent God representation.

Roberts (1989) used 10 adjectives that reflected polar opposites of God's nature (critical-accepting, demanding-giving, punishing-forgiving, frustrated-successful, serious-playful), listed them randomly and had participants rank each adjective separately on a scale from never (1) to always (5). Unlike Benson and Spilka's Loving God Index and Controlling God Index, he does not list adjectives in bipolar opposites. Participants can chose opposite adjectives if they wish, to more fully describe an ambivalent God representation. Phrases describing the same characteristics were used to ask participants how they saw themselves. Roberts was interested in the degree to which God was a projection of the self, that is, the correlation between God adjectives and self adjectives. He found, first, that God is imagined along two dimensions---as nurturing and/or disciplining. He also found that

> Subjects who often think of themselves as generous, sincere, or easy to "forgive and forget" and who seldom perceive themselves as hard to please or depressed are most likely to imagine a nurturing God. Subjects who describe themselves as suspicious of others' motives or as depressed are most likely to perceive God as disciplining. (Roberts, 1989, p. 379)

Women are more likely than men to perceive God as nurturing. Also, church attendance is positively associated with the nurturing image of God. Finally, poorer people perceived God as more disciplining than affluent people.

Roberts' 10 adjectives and two dimensional God representation constitute a measure of peoples' God representation. Roberts does not describe how, out of a multitude of adjectives, he chose the adjectives he did. There is no indication that he pooled adjectives from previous studies or from a norming group. It is not clear whether these adjectives best describe the dimensions of God representations.

Two studies utilize images of God data from the General Social Survey (1983). In 1983 this survey, distributed to a random number of participants throughout the United States, contained six bipolar adjectival pairs describing images of God. Nelsen, Cheek and Au (1985) subjected this data on the images of God to a factor analysis and identified three images of God: as king, healer and relational. Roof and Roof (1984) cross-tabulated data on the 12 images of God with several social and demographic factors. A difficulty with the item format of the images of God is their placement in bipolar pairs. Respondents must chose one or the other of a pair, for example, mother or father, instead of both dimensions. The adjectival bipolar pairs are also problematic in that they encompass only positive images of God and not negative images such as a punitive God. It is unfortunate that the items on God images were so poorly constructed since there is a wealth of research possibilities from such a large, random sample in terms of cross-tabulation between images of God and other factors.

The most extensively developed and used measure of God representations based on the semantic differential technique has been the Semantic Differential Parental Scale (the SDPS). The scale utilizes Vergote's (1981a, p. 17) distinction between the symbolic figures of parents and the memory images of parents. He hypothesizes that it is the symbolic images and not the memory images that make up the essential content of God representations. The effect of this hypothesis is that the God representation is symbolized through the ideals of father and mother and there is no allowance for God being symbolized through the negative imagery that may be part of memory images of parents. One way to understand Vergote's hypothesis is in terms of Spero's (1992) distinction between anthropocentric God representations created from internal representations of mother and father (the memory images) and deocentric God representations created from experiences of God as an external reality.

The SDPS, developed in Belgium and then translated into several languages including English, consists of 36 maternal and paternal attributes each of which is a unipolar seven point scale. Half of these items are most attributed to symbolic images of mother and half to father (in the studies used to norm the scale). Participants are asked to go through all 36 items three times, rating items in terms of symbolic mother, symbolic father and God. The data of the SDPS are analyzed in terms of mean intensity scores of attributes which indicate the degree to which maternal and paternal attributes are assigned to God. In 1972, Pasquali (1981) used American source texts and subjects to create a new English language version of the SDPS. The SDPS II has 72 items (36 paternal and 36 maternal).

The SDPS and SDPS II have been used in several studies with various age and cultural populations (Vergote & Tamayo, 1981). The general conclusion drawn from these studies is that while both maternal and paternal attributes are present in peoples' God representations, paternal attributes more adequately describe the God representation than maternal attributes (Vergote, 1981b).

There are several questions of validity which make the SDPS and SDPS II problematic to use. First, the <u>SDPS</u> and <u>SDPS II</u> were developed and normed with predominantly Roman Catholic samples. Consequently, they may be valid only with this population. One wonders whether the scale would have been constructed differently if a heterogenous religious sample had been used. The second most problematic aspect of the scale concerns the construct validity of Vergote's hypothesis that God representations are constructed solely from symbolic and not also from memory images of father and mother.

The <u>SDPS</u> and <u>SDPS II</u> are not useful for the purposes of this study, not simply because of questions of validity and construction but primarily because they do not yield a God representation that has both positive and negative aspects or as Rizzuto puts it, "full object representations in which multiple and even contradictory aspects of the object are simultaneously included" (Rizzuto, 1979, p. 57).

The Q-sort technique

The Q-sort technique was developed by Stephenson (1953). In this technique participants are given a set of cards containing adjectives or traits. They are asked to sort these into piles ranging from most characteristic to least characteristic of God. To ensure uniform distribution of ratings a "forced-normal" distribution is used, with participants being told to place a specified number of cards in each pile.

Nelson and Jones (1957) used a Q-sort procedure when they developed the <u>Q-test for Parent Deity</u>, in order to measure the relationship between descriptions of God, mother and father concepts. The instrument consists of 60 statements such as, "I have a sense of being protected," "I have a feeling that I am understood," "I have a feeling that this is someone who does not love me." Each statement is on a card and participants sort cards three times using three sentence stems: "When I think of father..."; "When I think of mother..."; and "When I think of God..." The sorting is done on a nine point scale, with an exact number of cards assigned for each point:

	<u>Most like I feel</u>						<u>Least like I feel</u>	
Scale:	0	1	2	3	4	5	6	7	8
# of cards:	1	2	6	12	18	12	6	2	1

The responses are scored by assigning the value on the scale as the score for each statement in that position. For each participant the score each statement had received when sorted for the God concept was correlated with the score each statement received when ranked for father and mother concepts.

Strunk (1959) used their scale with a homogeneous sample group of 20 male students and Godin and Hallez (1964) used a translation of the test with 70 French speaking Belgiums. Nelson (1971) hypothesized that the conflicting results of these studies (Nelson and Jones found that the concept of God more highly correlated with mother, Strunk with father, and Godin and Hallez with the preferred parent) supported the findings of Godin and Hallez and he tested this with a sample group of 87 participants. A limitation with the Q-test for Parent Deity is that the authors did not collect a wide sample of statements concerning God, father and mother concepts, thus it is not known whether all the dimensions of these concepts are represented.

In reviewing these studies Spilka, Armatas and Nussbaum (1964) suggested that when participants conceptualized images of mother, father, self and God in verbal terms socially desirable words were equivalently assigned to all while socially undesirable terms were avoided. In their study the authors also emphasized the need for a full range of imagery when constructing measures of God-representations and cited this as a weakness in previous studies. They attempted to develop a measure of God concepts which adequately sampled the population of appropriate concepts.

Using over 200 participants, they obtained a pool of answers to the question, "What does God mean to you?" Judges analyzed words that were commonly employed and easy to understand and read. These judgments resulted in a selection of 64 terms. These were combined in a Q-sort format. The internal consistency reliability coefficient estimated by Cronbach's alpha was .69 (Armatas, 1962).

The God-concept Q-sort, as the measure was called, was tested with a very religious group and a moderately religious group. The data for the 64 items were analyzed factorially and 12 factors comprising 91 percent of the total variance were extracted. The adjectives in each group made up a continuum, with positive factor loadings indicating which end of the continuum was being described in the grouping. The following lists summarize the factors for each group.

Very religious sample

1. Wrathful, avenging, and damning God
2. The stern father
3. Impersonal omni- or all-ness God concept:
    God as omnipresent, omnipotent, omniscient
4. Impersonal distant God, as opposed to one who might be close and human, with the all-ness feature of the preceding group.
5. God, the kindly father/earthly Christ

6. God as matchless and timeless (similar to group 3)
7. Impersonal, supreme ruler.
8. Blessed, gentle, holy God (as opposed to powerful and formal)
9. The spiritual-just God
10. The God of righteousness
11. The real, firm God

Moderately religious sample

1. Comforting, helpful, patient, warm, charitable and supporting God
2. Wrathful, avenging, damning God
3. Impersonal omni- or all-ness God concept
4. Kind and benevolent ruler
5. Impersonal, distant and mythical God who is permissive and nonrestrictive
6. A formal, democratic God who is unchanging and firm
7. Powerful, timeless father
8. Supreme ruler who is blessed and gentle
9. Strong and powerful God
10. Holy, guiding, forgiving God
11. Loving, glorious divine God
12. Matchless and unchanging God

The authors used the Edwards' Social Desirability Scale to test whether factors were correlated with social desirability. None of the correlations of God factors and social desirability were significant.

The authors were hesitant to match their factors across the two samples because of difficulties with making both factoral and conceptual comparisons. They concluded that different groups may possess varying God concepts and this may be a function of special religious training.

This study is important in that it tested whether people chose God concepts because of social desirability. Also, it used a large pool of adjectives describing God to construct the scale. It became a basis for developing further measures of God representations (Gorsuch, 1968).

The God-concept Q-sort has been used in several studies. Benson and Spilka (1973) selected 6 factors from the 11 factors found in the highly religious sample group. They used these to study the relationship between self esteem and God images, and locus of control and God images and found a significant correlation between self esteem and God images and a lack of correlation between locus of control and God images. They also developed the 13 item semantic differential scale to measure loving and controlling God images which was described earlier in the discussion of the semantic differential technique.

This study is of interest in the investigation of the relationship between traumatization and God representations, both as a model for a research design and also because of its findings. One would guess that traumatization affects self esteem and that there is a parallel between locus of control and traumatization. Locus of control is operationally defined with Rotter's (1966) 23 item scale that measures internal-external control. People who view themselves as the cause of their own behavior are said to have internal control while those who feel they are not masters of their own fate give control to an external source. One would suppose that those who have been traumatized would rate high in terms of external control, although this supposition may be problematic if people consciously are highly controlled as a way to compensate for unconscious feelings of their lives being out of their own control. It may be that such a locus of control scale is not useful in measuring the complexities of locus of control for those who have been traumatized.

Jolley and Taulbee (1986) build on the research of Benson and Spilka (1973), measuring the relationship between self concepts and conceptions of God in a group of students (normals) and prisoners (deviants). Their hypothesis was that Benson and Spilka's findings would be confirmed and that deviants (prisoners) would have a less positive self concept and conception of God than normals (students). In this study the authors only utilized the 13 item God concept scale developed by Benson and Spilka (1973) yielding scores for loving God and controlling God and they did not use other scales, as Benson and Spilka had done. The use of this scale is problematic, as was noted earlier, in terms of its construction and the pairing of adjectives which preclude multivalent God representations.

Factor analyses

Gorsuch (1968) used the God-concept Q-sort (Spilka, Armatas & Nussbaum, 1964) as his starting point for developing a new scale. He re-tested its factors and found four to five factors which matched across the two samples: the stern father, the omni-concept God, the impersonal God, the kindly father, and the supreme ruler. Gorsuch also utilized the semantic differential theory of the general meaning of concepts, suggesting that some of the factors found by Spilka and his colleagues corresponded to the three dimensions of meaning described by Osgood, Suci and Tannenbaum (1957). In his research he used a sample of people with a variety of religious and non-religious attitudes in order to see whether there were common factors in their God representations and whether these corresponded to the dimensions of meaning described by Osgood, Suci and Tannenbaum (1957).

Gorsuch added 23 adjectives from Osgood, Suci and Tannenbaum (1957) to the 63 used by Spilka, Armatas and Nussbaum (1964). He didn't use adjectives in pairs, but singly. He added eight random variables and one variable for sex, bringing the total number of adjectives to one hundred. He asked participants to rate adjectives on a three point scale: "1" meant the word does not describe God, "2" meant the word does describe God and "3" meant the word describes God particularly well.

The adjectives were rated by approximately 600 undergraduates, representing a wide variety of religious and non-religious attitudes. The factors were correlated across the sample and factored. Factor one (a third order factor) was the largest grouping, with 51 adjectives. Gorsuch describes this as the traditional Christian concept of God, "who is a deity and yet is actively concerned for and involved with mankind" (Gorsuch, 1968, p. 58). The next two factors were the interpretable second order factors, which Gorsuch labelled as benevolent deity (comforting, not distant, forgiving, not impersonal, not inaccessible, loving, merciful, not passive, protective and redeeming) and companionable (considerate, fair, faithful, helpful, kind, moving and warm). The eight primary factors of the first order analysis were labelled kindliness, wrathfulness, deisticness (so transcendent as to have little relationship with humanity), omni-ness, evaluation, irrelevancy, eternality, potently passive.

Comparing his results with those of Spilka, Armatas and Nussbaum (1964), Gorsuch states that three factors of the God concept can be firmly established and several others tentatively established. The former are the omni-ness factor, where adjectives chosen in Gorsuch's sample and Spilka's two samples are almost identical, deisticness (consistent across the three samples) and wrathfulness. Gorsuch found no factors which clearly matched the dimensions of meaning described by Osgood, Suci and Tannenbaum, although evaluation and potency seemed to be dimensions of several factors described in the study.

Gorsuch's scale has much to recommend it as an instrument for peoples' conscious God-representations. It utilizes a wide pool of adjectives and builds upon previous research, being tested with three large sample groups. He also tested for the internal consistency reliability of each factor scale. Gorsuch did not address issues of construct validity which can be raised in terms of theory of the semantic differential, but since he doesn't incorporate this theory into his scale, it doesn't affect its construct validity.

Several studies have selected out factors identified by Spilka, Armatas and Nussbaum (1964) and Gorsuch (1968) and used these to study particular dimensions of God representations. For example, Nelsen, Waldron and Stewart (1973) selected 17 items used in both tests which factored into the concepts of loving God and punitive God. They were testing the hypotheses that 1) sectarianism and the holding of an "Old Testament view of God as vindictive" are related, 2) religious attendance and the holding of an "Old Testament view of God" are unrelated and 3) holding a "New Testament image of God as helpful and merciful" is positively related to religious attendance. The difficulties of the study are twofold. First, the authors' labels of "Old Testament God and New Testament God" are simplistic in the polarity they create and do not account for the richness of God imagery in either Hebrew or Christian scriptures. This point is made by Potvin (1977) in his review of the literature on God representation measures and supported in his research, showing that adolescents understand God as both loving and punishing. Also, the use of just two factors may not do justice to the richness of God imagery that may be present among sectarians and those who attend worship.

In a study of the correlations between mother, father, self and God concepts Spilka, Addison and Rosensohn (1975) used both the 13 item semantic differential scale developed by Benson and Spilka (1973) to measure loving God and controlling God images and Gorsuch's Adjective Ratings of God Scale, utilizing the factors of wrathful God, traditional God image, kindliness God image, Omniness God image, and Deisticness God image. The most interesting finding of this study is that males and females differ significantly in terms of correlations between self, God, mother and father concepts. While males had three significant correlations between father and God concepts, females had only one. None of the mother-God associations were significant for males, while among females there were five significant correlations between mother and God concepts. Also, among females there was a significant correlation between preferred parent and God concept, while this was not so for males. Previous studies do not attend to gender differences. This study, done in 1975, points to gender differences highlighted in feminist developmental theory. The authors suggest, in closing their study, that the measures available for describing God, parent and self concepts may be too restricting in terms of the limited dimensions described.

Hammersla, Andrews-Qualls and Frease (1986) modified Gorsuch's Adjective Ratings of God Scale in their study of 542 students at a Christian college. They added 27 items and deleted 37 items. A five point scale instead of a three point scale was used by respondents. The adjectives were not factor analyzed. Instead they were combined into six subscales, reportedly based on Gorsuch's factors and the six factors selected by Benson and Spilka (1973) in their modification of Gorsuch's scale. It is difficult to ascertain the exact correspondence between the six scales constructed here and Gorsuch's factors, since there has been considerable modification. The authors also added three new scales, to cover what they saw as omissions in earlier studies. A sensual God scale was constructed and its validity was based upon conversations with students and recent literature "from the 'new' religious consciousness" (Hammersla et al., 1986, p.

426). A creative God scale and a valuable God scale were constructed with some of Gorsuch's adjectives and added ones.

The difficulty with such a radical modification of Gorsuch's factors is that the authors do not undertake a factor analysis of the new set of 90 adjectives, presuming that they "load" unto the factors they have identified. This may or may not be the case. Without a factor analysis they are not able to determine that there are nine separate scales as they have identified them. Some of these scales may overlap with others and thus the scores from each are not valid for measuring separate dimensions of God representations. Indeed, the authors found that high correlations among the scales suggest four dimensions, not the nine identified in the scales. The first is a favorable God dimension (comprising the six positive aspect scales) and an unfavorable God dimension (the irrelevant God scale), a vindictive dimension and a distant dimension.

Wootton (1990), similar to Hammersla et al. (1986), revised the same two instruments, the God-Concept Q-sort (Spilka et al., 1964) and the Adjective Ratings of God Scale (Gorsuch, 1968). He began with four characterizations of God: omni-ness, deisticness, wrathfulness and traditional Christian. He dropped the first, concluding that it was too abstract and indefinable (Wootton, 1990, p. 68). He renamed the remaining characterizations as loving God (traditional Christian), absent God (deisticness) and wrathful God. Wootton noted that there is ample support in literature and religious theory to support these three dimensions of God.

Wootton added a fourth characterization, that of an observing God "who is good but not as active and strong as the Loving God" (Wootton, 1990, p. 71). The existence of this characterization in the literature on God representations is well supported (Rizzuto, 1979, p. 91; and Meissner, 1984, p. 155). He surmised that this characterization did not emerge in the factor analytic studies because of the original selection of adjectives.

Wootton (1990, p. 72) described the interrelationships of these God representations:

> Loving God--benevolent and active
> Observing God--benevolent and passive
> Absent God--malevolent and passive
> Wrathful God--malevolent and active.

In constructing his measures Wootton selected items from Gorsuch's list of adjectives that had high factor loadings on his original factors of "Wrathfulness," "Deisticness" and "traditional Christian" and added synonyms so that there were three equally numbered lists of adjectives. He added a fourth list of words depicting the observing God characterization. He utilized a group of five raters to rank the adjectives on each list for how well each evoked the appropriate characterization. There were 20 items for each scale. Wootton called this measure the Adjective Characterization of God Task (ACGT). Participants rate adjectives according to whether they (1) do not, (2) do describe and (3) describe God particularly well.

He devised a second measure, called the Wootton Metaphor Characterization of God Task (WMCGT) utilizing the Q-sort technique. Wootton hypothesized that metaphors would access peoples' inner images of God and that metaphors are mediated by more perceptual associations, while adjectives are mediated by the structures of verbal associations. Wootton constructed the WMCGT by generating lists of metaphors for each of the four characterizations of God. This was done by a committee and from popular and religious literature. Five raters judged how well the metaphors fit the four characterizations of God. The number of metaphors on each scale was limited to 15. The metaphors were put on 60 cards which participants Q-sorted.

In a third instrument, the Wootton Adjusted Ranking Characterization God Task (WARCGT) participants were asked to rank the four characterizations of God according to how well each corresponded with their own relationship with God. After ranking these, from one to four, they were asked to say how far apart the four characterizations were relative to one another and in comparison with their own private image of God.

Wootton used the scales with a sample of 101 undergraduates. He found that means for the loving God scale ranked first across the three measures and there was considerable variance across the three instruments in the comparative rankings of the three remaining scales (Wootton, 1990, p. 115). He used three multitrait-multimethod matrices to review the bivariate correlational analyses among the three instruments, as a way of investigating whether the scales were assessing similar or overlapping constructs. He found that the loving and wrathful scales are supported as valid categories, while the observing and absent scales are not (Wootton, 1990, p. 186).

Wootton found that the observing God of the WMCGT is less benevolent and more malevolent than the absent God. The WMCGT appeared to describe "the abandoning and unapproachable aspect of a detached and remote other" rather than "the soothing and comforting aspect of being observed" (Wootton, 1990, p. 183). Wootton speculated that the metaphors constructed by the writing committee who assisted in constructing the instrument may describe repressed aspects of being observed which are less comforting than conscious aspects.

Similarly, the absent God scale of the <u>WMCGT</u> was not significantly related to any of the scales of the <u>ACGT</u> or the <u>WARCGT</u>, suggesting that a different dimension of absence was tapped. This absence was not malevolent, as expected, but more "evocative of a yearning for peace and solitude than of the experience of separation or remoteness" (Wootton, 1990, p. 184). The observing God and absent God scales of the <u>WMCGT</u> differ in correlational patterns from all the other correlational patterns obtained from comparing the scales across the three measures. Wootton wondered whether this was due to 1) shortcomings in the construction of the instruments, or whether 2) the categories of "observing" and "absent" are less powerful and distinct as "loving" and "wrathful." A third reason could be that they were not valid dimensions of the God representations of the young adults who made up the sample. A fourth reason might be that the scales of the <u>WMCGT</u> may have tapped into levels not so easily characterized as positive or negative:

> The experience of being observed by God may be comforting at one level and disturbing at another. In the same way the experience of separation from God may admit of a similar ambivalence of feelings, thoughts, and images across levels. (Wootton, 1990, p. 188)

This may be because "metaphors may tap images that are not fully conscious or, at least, not capable of conscious verbalization" (Wootton, 1990, p. 189). Wootton concludes

> It may be the case that the <u>WMCGT</u>, among the dependent variable measures, was the most attuned to the level of "unconscious processes" in the assessment of the God-representation and, therefore, more sensitive than the <u>ACGT</u> or <u>WARCGT</u> to the repressed but influential images in the memorial matrix. (Wootton, 1990, p. 194)

Replication and further studies of convergent and discriminant validity are needed to support this conclusion.

Wootton's development of these instruments builds upon the work of Gorsuch (1968) and Spilka et al. (1964). His comprehensive review of the literature allows him to avoid shortcomings of many previously developed instruments: in particular, the lack of negative adjectives and the bipolar formatting of items which do not allow for ambiguous imagery of God. His use of metaphors is an innovative addition to the instruments and may be able to draw upon unconscious sources of God representations. Finally, his use of committees and rankers ensures that a wide pool of adjectives and metaphors will be assembled and that there will be some consensus on which adjectives and metaphors most describe God in the four characterizations Wootton uses.

In summation, I concur with Wootton's (1990) conclusion that there are no standardized or even widely used instruments for measuring God representations. Since instruments, when used in successive studies, have been adapted to the needs of each investigation, there is no pool of studies utilizing the same instrumentation. Wootton's three measures of God representation have scales for loving and wrathful God representations that have been shown to be valid. The questions raised concerning the absent and observing God scales point more to the need for further investigation, rather than to abandoning these scales. I will be using Wootton's three measures, the WMCGT, the ACGT and the WARCGT as he did, with the four scales on each measuring loving, observing, absent and wrathful representations. Like Wootton, I will use three multitrait-multimethod matrices to review the bivariate correlational analyses among the three instruments, to see if the results from this sample support Wootton's findings that the observing and absent God representation scales of the WMCGT differ in their correlational patterns from the patterns obtained from the other scales and measures.

Studies on Correlations between Traumatization and God Representations

Pastoral theologians, psychologists and psychotherapists assume that at the deepest level of personality are structures that express and define one's faith and value system. Browning (1991) calls this the visional-obligational dimension of the personality, expressed in the narratives and metaphors used to describe one's self, God and the world. The types of God representations (for example, loving, observing, absent, wrathful) can be considered as "existential codes" (Kundera, 1988, p. 29) which underlie the story of who we are. From a cognitive developmental perspective, these types of God representations shape the complex cognitive schemata of self, others and God. Traumatization can temporarily generate its own series of existential codes, to do with badness, danger, disintegration, paralysis, rage, terror. When traumatic stressors are recurrent, such existential codes become embedded in one's narrative and may be inter-related to one's belief system and representations of God.

The underlying themes generated in traumatization become the underpinnings for cognitive schemata. McCann and Pearlman (1990, pp. 62-78) have elaborated the ways in which complex schemata are disrupted during traumatization. These schemata concern one's frame of reference to the world, safety, trust/dependency, independence, power, esteem, and intimacy. Implicit in all of these are underlying God representations. For example, belief in safety and invulnerability may accompany representations of God as benevolent, loving and protective. When these beliefs are shattered in traumatization then God may be experienced as absent.

> Traumatized people feel utterly abandoned, utterly alone, cast out of the
> human and divine systems of care and protection that sustain life.
> (Herman, 1992, p. 52)

When schemata of independence and power are disrupted in traumatization, these
may lead to shifts in representations of God. Complex religious systems in which
God is all-powerful and the person is dependent and powerless may take shape as
a means of putting an all-powerful God in place of the assailant who was
overpowering (Fairbairn, 1952).

The inter-relationship between traumatization and cognitive schemata has
been demonstrated empirically (Janoff-Bulman, 1989a). Using an instrument
called the World Assumptions Scale, Janoff-Bulman demonstrated that victims
were significantly different from nonvictims in terms of 1) their tendency to view
themselves less positively, 2) their belief in the world as random, and 3) their
view that the interpersonal world is less benevolent and more malevolent.
Underlying these attitudes of oneself as unworthy, the world as random, and the
interpersonal world as malevolent may be representations of God as absent and/or
wrathful.

A study of Holocaust survivors demonstrated that they and their children
described themselves as religious more often than a control group (Carmil &
Breznitz, 1991). Do these findings contradict Janoff-Bulman's? Would someone
who described oneself as religious also view oneself less positively, see the world
as random and the interpersonal world as malevolent? It is difficult to compare
these findings, both in terms of how Janoff-Bulman's world assumptions
correspond with describing oneself as religious, and also in terms of traumatic
stressors, that is, comparing the Holocaust to whatever traumatic stressors were
experienced by Janoff-Bulman's sample.

The metaphor of trauma as God can be used to describe the way both
traumatic experiences and religious experiences are characterized by an inability
to absorb the impact of the traumatic or religious event because it is
overwhelming:

> Just as God has been described as transcendent and unknowable, a trauma
> is an event which transcends our capacity to experience it. Compared to
> the finite nature of the traumatized soul, the traumatic event seems
> infinite, all-powerful, and wholly other. (Mogenson, 1989, p. 1-2)

Traumatic stressors are overwhelming because we have no metaphors with which to understand what is happening.[10] In other words, traumatic stressors, with their life-threatening quality, make nonsense of our ultimate metaphors, that the world is a safe place and that we will be taken care of when in danger.

> To stand before an event for which we have no metaphors is to stand in the tabernacle of the Lord. Like Moses before the bush that burned and yet was not consumed, the soul falls down prostrate before whatever it is unable to relativize into images. (Mogenson, 1989, p. 7)

Studies of the religion of people with multiple personality disorders show that such individuals often come from homes where fundamentalist Christianity and strict religious practices are combined with severe punishments and emotional or sexual repression (Gottlieb, 1977; Saltman & Solomon, 1982). Multiple personality disorder always arises in the context of severe abuse. Understanding the religious history and belief systems of this population can shed light on the relationship between trauma and God representations. The two factors of severe abuse and fundamentalist religions may make this population especially susceptible to God representations which are shaped by traumatic experiences. Similarly, the use of scripture to justify severe corporal punishment from an early age, as has been so prevalent in some Protestant families and religious communities (Greven, 1990) may intrapsychically fuse memories of physical abuse with God representations. In the intrapsychic world of such physically abused children, representations of God may be associated with fear, pain, rigorous control, breaking the will, submission and obedience.

Coons (1980) found that among multiple personality clients who found religion important, one personality frequently espoused a fundamentalist religion while another personality was atheistic or rebelled against religion. Bowman, Coons, Jones and Oldstrom (1987) found that among seven clients with multiple personalities, five clients experienced their relationship with God as ambivalent. For them, God was personal, intense, and ever present but in both a benevolent and wrathful way. This paralleled their experience of their parents. Indeed, their images of God were both of a benevolent God who carried their idealized parent imago and of an angry, demanding God who carried the image of the severely punitive superego. In this client group, secondary personalities carried feelings of anger towards God, parents, and religion. The authors concluded that God images were correlated with the object relations of personalities and reflected the dynamics of parental object relations. Bowman (1989, p. 234), in commenting

---

[10]One way to understand this lack of metaphors may be to think of traumatization as collapsing the transitional space, the "as if" space that Winnicott links with the imagination and culture. Terr (1990) describes post-traumatic play of children as a literal re-enactment of traumatization. Such children, when drawing upon traumatic memories, can only repeat the literal events, with no quality of pretend or real play.

on her work with clients, said that the personalities in a multiple personality disorder "who cannot believe in God are often those who experienced abuse and have connected God with hated parental images." This study illustrates how traumatic stressors of abuse by parents can shape God representations in people with multiple personalities.

Fundamentalism may be an overlooked factor in the etiology of multiple personality disorder. Higdon and Faheem (1984) suggest that a literal interpretation of scripture may contribute to the splitting of ambivalence and the repression from consciousness of unacceptable thoughts or feelings, and the forming of a severely punitive superego. Fundamentalism may be part of difficulties in cognitive development that occurred at the time of traumatization: in particular, inflexibility in organized schemata and cognitive structures (Fish-Murray, Koby and van der Kolk, 1987).

Fairbairn (1952) described a way of coping with the internalized bad object of the sexual abuser. Commenting that children as victims identified with such a bad object, Fairbairn went on to describe "the moral defense" against such a bad object. The object internalized by the child is bad and in as much as the child identifies with such an object he or she is unconditionally bad. The child can evade unconditional badness by internalizing good objects, which assume a super-ego role. Then the child has simply to cope with conditional badness and goodness: both conditional on the moral rulings of the superego. Fairbairn described the internal scenario in religious terms:

> It is better to be a sinner in a world ruled by God than to live in a world ruled by the Devil. A sinner in a world ruled by God may be bad; but there is always a certain security to be derived from the fact that the world around is good---'God's in His heaven---All's right with the world!'; and in any case there is always the hope of redemption. In a world ruled by the Devil the individual may escape the badness of being a sinner; but he is bad because the world around him is bad. Further, he can have no sense of security and no hope of redemption. The only prospect is one of death and destruction. (Fairbairn, 1952, pp. 66-67)

Fairbairn's theory can be elaborated using Spero's distinction between anthropocentric and deocentric God representations (Spero, 1992). Fairbairn is describing internal anthropocentric God representations which are pieced together from internalized human object representations that have coalesced during traumatization. These anthropocentric God representations are then projected onto the external environment and may also be embedded in religious systems involving unconditional badness, grace, redemption and forgiveness. When one's religious culture also depicts parents as honorable, the self as bad, God as distant and condemning, and abuse as deserved punishment, then such a culture acts as a "modificatory mechanism" (Spero, 1992, p. 138) that further shapes and reinforces the religious system, God and self representations described by Fairbairn. Both the individual and the culture project such God representations onto the world.

Children raised in strict, Protestant homes where corporal punishment is understood as a God-given means of child-rearing will internalize the religious systems of their parents and religious community. Biographies and autobiographies written by Protestant evangelists often describe the horrible experience of corporal punishment and justify the distorted faith systems of abusing parents: faith systems which depict an overpowering God who demands obedience through fear and the infliction of pain (Greven, 1990). This God becomes internally linked with a "monstrous superego that devours life instead of transforming it" (Vergote, 1988, p. 62). Benevolent ordering and law from parents is linked with harsh judgment and punishment. Certainly, in the chaos of trauma, particularly child abuse, and in the harshness of parents who use abuse as "discipline," such a superego is formed and may be transformed into an image of God.

When the dimensions of kindness, distance and wrathfulness of God and parental representations were measured among abused and non abused children, Johnson and Eastburg (1992) found no differences in the God concepts of abused and nonabused children, while abused children described parents as less kind and more wrathful than nonabused children. Among all of the children, God was often viewed as simultaneously kind, wrathful and distant, while the parental representations were not multidimensional; that is, in parental representations distance was not combined with either kindness or wrathfulness. The multivalent God representation described by many of these children has the potential to develop in at least three directions. Under extreme abuse, it could split, like the God representations of those with multiple personalities. In the aftermath of abuse, it could form the religious defense described by Fairbairn where the self carries the badness associated with abuse and God remains kind and distant and potentially wrathful. In a nurturing, healing environment, such a multivalent God representation could carry the depth, mystery and range of a complex, contradictory God representation that was not simplistic and uni-dimensional.

Justice and Lambert (1986) found that adult patients who report histories of sexual abuse also report more negative God images than patients who do not report a history of sexual abuse. Linking this study with Johnson and Eastburg's (1992), one could conclude that the multivalent God representations in childhood become more negative in adulthood among those who were sexually abused.

In surveys and interviews of women who experienced incest in childhood, such women describe themselves as alienated from the Judeo-Christian religious traditions of their childhood (Poling, 1992; Imbens & Jonker, 1992). Karen, a survivor of sexual violence, writes

> Am I angry at God, or the people who make up the church? My feelings towards God are numb. I confess I fear God. I feel very much alone and wonder if there is a loving God out there for me. (Poling, 1992, p. 47)

In a Dutch study of the correlation between a religious upbringing and the sexual abuse of girls within Christian families, Imbens and Jonker's (1992) interviewed nineteen women. All but one of the Roman Catholic women and all of the Protestant women said they have turned their backs on the church of their childhood. Each woman was asked to describe her image of God. God was described as all seeing and all-powerful, a being who didn't intervene in the abuse because "I was a bad girl who deserved to be punished" (Imbens & Jonker, 1992, p. 33). God was like the abusing father "with such almighty power that it's frightening" (Imbens & Jonker, 1992, p. 41). The themes of God being all powerful, all knowing, punitive, and frightening run throughout the interviews. God is described as loving by five women, however these loving images of God are mostly associated with Jesus.

> During the period these women experienced incest, they primarily experienced Jesus as loving, good, human, and close. He was closer than God, more pleasant, less judgmental, less strict, and less powerful. (Imbens & Jonker, 1992, p. 211)

Given the cultural differences between Johnson and Eastburg's (1992) sample of American children and Imbens and Jonker's (1992) sample of Dutch women, it is difficult to compare their findings. Had these Dutch women been asked as children to describe God, would God have been multivalent---kindly, distant, and wrathful---as God was for the American children? And will the abused children in Johnson's and Eastburg's study become adults who describe God primarily as punitive, all-powerful and frightening? Longitudinal studies are needed to answer such questions.

In a study of the autobiographical literature of Protestant evangelicals who experienced physical abuse in childhood, Greven (1990) illustrates how often these individuals affirm both loving and wrathful representations of a God who uses fear and the threat of punishment to obtain obedience. Given that nearly all of these autobiographies are about men, one could speculate that gender may be a crucial factor in determining whether adults embrace or reject a God who resembles the abuser. The men described in the autobiographies reviewed by Greven for the most part identify God as all-powerful, all-good, and punitive. In their endorsement of corporal punishment they align themselves as parents with such a God.

Individuals who cope with traumatization through rigid God representations may find some sort of relief in preserving their parental and God representations as good, and in creating a world where strict punitive laws order life. For example, they may come to rely on God representations of an omnipotent, judging, punitive God consonant with rigid fundamentalist religions.[11] Such rigid religious systems may serve as a protection against the primitive imagery of abuse which is experienced as demonic. In ego psychological terms, the regression to the helpless ego state that occurred during traumatization may constellate an image of an all powerful God who may consciously be experienced as protective but unconsciously as destructive and threatening.

Pastoral psychotherapists often work with individuals who adopt a fundamentalist, rigid religious system as a way of coping with overwhelming life experiences.[12] Just as psychologists understand how the "freezing" of the traumatic material is a necessary step at a time when such material cannot be processed, pastoral psychologists understand how a rigid fundamentalist religion may be a necessary step in recovery. If recovery is able to proceed, then individuals may simultaneously begin to unfreeze both traumatic material and their rigid, fixed religious systems.

Such an understanding of the relationship between trauma and fixed, rigid religious cognitive schemata may be highlighted when we are able to measure the impact of traumatic stressors on God representations. Further research, beyond the scope of this dissertation, might highlight how limited, fixed or rigid God representations[13] will likely go hand in hand with a psychological system in which traumatic material is fixed in a frozen mass. These rigid, fixed God

---

[11]In Fish-Murray, Koby and van der Kolk's study (1987) comparing severely abused children with non-abused children, they found that severely abused children showed inflexibility in cognitive schemata and had markedly different concepts of justice in which rules were made and punishable by the largest male. We can hear an implicit image of an overpowering, punishing male God in this concept.

[12]Bradford (1990, p. 38), in a study comparing the psychologies of early Christian martyrs with individual cases involving borderline personality disorders, suicide and self mutilation, notes that "distinctions between normal and abnormal religiousness are not easily made... Distinguishing normal from abnormal religiousness may require analysis of such psychologically subtle matters as phenomenology of body image."

[13]The assumption I am working with is that rigid, limited God representations represent a lower or frozen level of development, while flexible, complex God representations correspond to a higher level of development. Rizzuto (1979, p. 57) states, "It is only at the highest level of our functioning, when secondary processes prevail persistently, that we deal with full object representations in which multiple, and even contradictory, aspects of the object are simultaneously included."

representations may have been used to cope with traumatic stressors through, as Mogenson suggests, subsuming one transcendent event (the trauma) under another (the unknowable God).

Summary

In reviewing the literature on traumatization I began by describing how traumatic stressors have an impact on core structures of the personality and how this impact could be measured.   A review of the literature on empirical measurement of traumatization demonstrated that the best available measure of traumatization for the purposes of this study is the Traumatic Antecedents Questionnaire.

The complexities of representations and God representations in particular were evident in reviewing this literature, and the most comprehensive model for understanding God representations involved an integration of object relations theory and cognitive developmental theory, in that God representations can be understood as a deep structural level which gives rise to complex cognitive schemata of God, self and others.   Reviewing empirical measurements of representations demonstrated that, while many innovative measures are being developed for exploring more unconscious dimensions of the representational world, these have not been used to look specifically at God representations.   The best available God representation measures are those developed by Wootton (1990).

CHAPTER THREE

METHODOLOGY

Hypotheses

As the review of literature has highlighted, theoretical and clinical literature on traumatization and God representations can be synthesized into a structural model in which the inter-relationship of traumatization and God representations generates complex cognitive schemata of self, God and the world. As a first step in demonstrating this model, I have designed a quantitative study of the inter-relationship of severity of traumatization and four God representations (loving, observing, absent and wrathful) in which these four hypotheses will be tested:

1) A positive relationship is hypothesized between wrathful God representations and traumatization: as traumatization increases, scores on the wrathful God representations will increase.

2) A positive relationship is hypothesized between absent God representations and traumatization: as traumatization increases, scores on absent God representations will increase.

3) A negative relationship is hypothesized between loving God representations and traumatization: as traumatization increases, scores on loving God representations will decrease.

4) A negative relationship is hypothesized between observing God representations and traumatization: as traumatization increases, scores on observing God representations will decrease.

Sample

Participants were drawn from graduate studies programs in social work, theology and psychology at a large university in the northeastern United States. They were approached in three ways: through bulletin board notices, announcements and graduate student mailboxes. Announcements and letters emphasized the fact that I wanted to interview both women who had memories of abuse and those who didn't. Replies were received from 138 women. The first 60 of these were contacted. These potential participants were informed of the nature of the study, the possible risks and benefits, and that the process would involve a one and a half hour interview. They were asked the question, "I want you to think about your childhood and adolescence and whether there were experiences you would describe as physical abuse, sexual abuse or witnessing domestic violence; if you were to describe the severity of this abuse on a scale from one to ten, how would you describe your experience?" This simple self report gave a rough indication of severity of traumatization and was used as a way to select the sample to include a spectrum of degrees of traumatization (as consciously remembered), from none to severe. The 47 participants were selected to balance the sample among the categories of no traumatization, traumatization, high traumatization and severe traumatization. They were paid a 20 dollar honorarium for participating in the study.

The sample consisted of 47 female participants, ranging in age from 21 to 58. Their average age was 30 years. Approximately half of the sample was 30 years and younger; 25 percent of the sample were between the ages of 30 and 40; while the remaining 25 percent were between the ages of 40 and 58. These participants were from the graduate studies programs in social work, theology and psychology at a large, co-educational private university, situated in a metropolitan area of the Northeast. About half of the participants (49 percent of the sample) were from the School of Theology; 15 (32 percent of the sample) were from the School of Social Work; and 9 (19 percent of the sample) were from the Department of Psychology.

Most of the participants (40) were white, with three Black participants, three Asian participants and one Hispanic participant. The majority (28) identified themselves presently as Protestant, 9 as having no religious affiliation, 5 as Roman Catholic, 3 as Jewish, 1 as Hindu and 1 as Buddhist. Childhood religion was described by 25 as Protestant, by 13 as Roman Catholic, by 5 as Jewish, by 2 as "none", by 1 as Hindu and 1 as Buddhist.

Measures

Severity of Traumatization

The variable, degree of traumatization, was measured using the Traumatic Antecedents Questionnaire developed by Herman and van der Kolk (1990). They devised a scoring procedure for assessing the severity of traumatic stressors of sexual abuse, physical abuse and witnessing domestic violence which they described in a study on childhood trauma (Herman, Perry & van der Kolk, 1989). They used a three by three matrix in scoring for positive indices of trauma (Table 1).

Table 1

Scoring Matrix for the Traumatic Antecedent Questionnaire

Type of Violence	Childhood (0 - 6)	Latency (7 - 12)	Adolescence (13 - 18)
Physical Abuse			
Sexual Abuse			
Witnessing Domestic Violence			

A score of zero was given in each of the three developmental stages if no abuse or witnessing domestic violence occurred. A score of one was given if such trauma did occur, with no distinction in scoring made within each developmental stage between single and repeated episodes of abuse by the same person. Additional scores of one were given in each developmental stage for abuse by different perpetrators. Thus, there was a range of scores from zero to nine, with higher scores for multiple perpetrators.

Physical abuse was defined as hitting, slapping, spanking and hitting with an object that was excessive, and more than an infrequent and mild form of punishment. Physical abuse included behavior such as being locked in a closet. Sexual abuse was defined as any sexual contact with someone at least five years older (fondling, masturbation, genital contact) before the victim was sixteen. Sexual play between equals was not defined as abuse and consensual sexual contact between adolescents who were equals was not defined as abuse. Clearly coercive and assaultive sexual contact before the age of eighteen was also included. When there was some question of whether the sexual contact was abusive, I explored with the participant how upsetting the experience was and how she would describe the impact of the sexual experience on her life. Domestic violence was defined as hitting, slapping, punching, and hitting with an object between parents or a parent and cohabitating partner.

God Representations

Four types of God representations were measured utilizing Wootton's (1990) three methods. In the Wootton Metaphor Characterization of God Task (WMCGT), the 60 metaphors (15 for each representation) were sorted by participants into seven rows, 3 in the first and last rows, 7 in the second and sixth rows, 12 in the third and fifth rows and 16 in the middle row. The rows towards the left were most like participants' images of God, and towards the right, least like participants' images of God, with the three metaphors at either end being the three most and least like their image of God. Participants sorted 60 metaphor cards into these columns and when they were done, recorded the number on each card into the corresponding position on a diagram. These were then coded by the scorer as loving, observing, absent or wrathful metaphors. The 3 metaphors most like their image of God were given scores of seven each, the next 7 were scored six each; the next 12, five each, and so on down to the last 3, scored one each. The possible range of scores for each representation was from 88 to 32.

The Adjective Characterization of God Task (ACGT) consisted of 80 adjectives (20 for each representation) that were rated by participants as three (describes God especially well), two (describes God) or one (does not describe God). These were scored by simply assigning the rating value to the type of God representation described by the adjective, with a range of scores from 60 (where all 20 adjectives of one representation were rated as "describes God especially well") to 20 (where all 20 adjectives of one representation were rated as "does not describe God").

The Wootton Adjusted Ranking Characterization of God Task (WARCGT) was scored by using the continuum from 10 (most like) to 0 (least like) on which participants had ranked the four characterizations of God. Scores were simply the number on the continuum where participants had placed each representation, with the possible scores ranging from 10 to 0.

Social Desirability

The third variable, social desirability, was measured by using the Marlowe Crowne Scale for Social Desirability (Crowne & Marlowe, 1960). The 34 true-false statements were scored by adding up the answers that presented individuals in a socially desirable fashion. The possible range of scores was from 0 to 34.

Additional Variables

An additional variable that was measured with the Traumatic Antecedents Questionnaire was whether participants described their parent or parents as alcoholic in their childhood.[1] This nominal variable was scored one for no alcoholism and two for alcoholism.

Another variable of interest from the Traumatic Antecedents Questionnaire was how participants described the role of religion in their current life and in their upbringing. This nominal variable was scored one for the answer "religion plays/played a minor role in my life/upbringing," two for "a major positive role," three for "a major negative role" and four for "a major role that was both negative and positive."

Procedure

Individual appointments were arranged for each interview. Participants were told that they would be asked to think about their "images of God" and also that there would be an extensive interview which would cover a description of primary caretakers and other important relationships in childhood and adolescence; major separations, moves and losses; sibling and peer relationships; family discipline and conflict resolution; family alcoholism; domestic violence; and physical and sexual abuse. The risks and benefits of participating in the study were reiterated, with an emphasis on the risk that their memories of abuse might resurface in the form of flashbacks. The interviewer reviewed with the participant what support systems were available to her if she was troubled after the interview. The informed consent form was reviewed and signed.

In the interview, the three measures of God representations and the Marlowe Crowne scale measuring social desirability were completed first. Then the

---

[1] In Section 6 on the Traumatic Antecedents Questionnaire there is a series of questions on family alcoholism. These questions are detailed enough to allow for an elaborate self report of a family member's use of alcohol, such that the interviewer was able to rate a parent as alcoholic or not alcoholic.

Traumatic Antecedents Questionnaire was used in a structured interview.

Data Analyses

The relationship between traumatization and loving, observing, absent and wrathful God representations was analyzed in several ways. First, a correlational matrix of mean scores of God representations and traumatization was used to determine the significance and direction of the relationship between severity of traumatization and each God representation. Next, a multiple regression was used to determine how much each God representation contributed uniquely to the overall correlation between God representations and severity of traumatization. Finally, women were divided into four trauma groups and a repeated measures analysis of variance (ANOVA) was used to compare the God representations of each group. A post hoc test (Fisher's LSD test) was used to evaluate the significance of the differences in mean scores of God representations between the four trauma groups.

Repeated measures analyses of variance were used in analyses of other significant correlations: the relationship between parent's alcoholism and God representations; ethnic group and God representations; and finally, the role of religion in childhood and God representations.

Since this is only the second research project using Wootton's three God representation tasks, I also evaluated convergent and discriminant validity of the God representation scales, using the multimethod-multitrait program of analysis developed by Campbell and Fiske (1959). To accomplish this, the correlational matrix of all God Representation scales was used in four ways. First, in the heterotrait-monomethod triangle of correlations, I considered the significance and direction of correlations among the different God representations (loving, observing, absent and wrathful) in each of the three measures (Metaphor, Adjective and Adjusted Ranking). Second, in the monotrait-heteromethod triangles I looked at the significance and direction of correlations between each type of God representation (loving, absent, observing and wrathful) across the three different methods. Third, I determined whether monotrait correlations (correlations between the same type of God representation as measured by different methods) were higher than correlations between the same God representation and different types of God representations in one method. Fourth, I considered whether patterns of inter-relationships between types of God representation were the same within and across methods.

CHAPTER FOUR

RESULTS

Descriptive Analyses of Demographic and Religious Variables

The sample was described in terms of age, religion and area of study at the beginning of the third chapter. Of interest is the portion of women who reported having no present religious identification (19 percent). In a recent national survey, 39 percent of those interviewed said that they had no current religious identification (Wright, 1990); that is, two times the percentage in my sample. This may indicate that my research project attracted more women who had current religious identifications than women who had no current religious identification.

As well, the high percentages of Protestant (60 percent), Caucasian (85 percent) participants may tend to limit the findings to this group. Socio-economic status can be assessed through the educational level of the participants' parents. Approximately 28 percent described their fathers as having Bachelor's degrees and 23 percent described their mothers as having Bachelor's degree, as compared with the national average of 24 percent and 17 percent respectively. Since this sample group was just slightly above the average national socio-economic status, the findings of this research will not be limited by socio-economic factors in terms of its generalizability.

Descriptive Analyses of Severity of Traumatization

Severity of traumatization, as measured using the scoring procedures for the Traumatic Antecedents Questionnaire, yielded scores from 0 (no conscious history of trauma) to 9 (traumatic episodes of several types spanning several developmental stages with possibly several perpetrators), with one participant having an extreme score of 18 (experiences of physical abuse, sexual abuse, and witnessing domestic violence in every developmental stage with a number of different perpetrators). The mean was 2.7, with a standard deviation of 3.3 and a range from 0 to 18.

No (conscious) memories of physical abuse, sexual abuse or witnessing domestic violence were reported by 15 participants (32 percent), with 13 participants (28 percent) describing memories of one type of violence by a single perpetrator in one developmental stage. Table 2 describes the range of traumatic experiences, as measured by the Traumatic Antecedents Questionnaire.

Table 2

Range of Scores on the Traumatic Antecedents Questionnaire

Number of Participants	Percentage of Participants	Score on the Traumatic Antecedents Questionnaire
15	32%	0
13	28%	1
2	4%	2
7	15%	3
2	4%	4
1	2%	5
2	4%	6
3	7%	7
1	2%	9
1	2%	18

For the purposes of some of the statistical analyses the sample was divided into four groups.[1] Scores of zero were grouped together and labelled No Traumatization (15 participants, 32 percent). Scores of one and two were grouped together and labelled Traumatized (15 participants, 32 percent). Scores of three and four were grouped together and labelled Highly Traumatized (9

---

[1]Dividing the sample into trauma groups was not part of the planned research design. The decision to subdivide the sample into trauma groups was made when it became clear that there was a correlation, but it was not linear. A repeated measures analysis of variance with trauma groups was a means of further exploring the correlation between severity of traumatization and God representations.

participants, 19 percent). Scores of five and over were grouped together and labelled Severely Traumatized (8 participants, 17 percent) (see Table 3).

Tables 4, 5, and 6 show the ages and types of trauma for each woman who reported trauma. Each number refers to one woman. So, for example, the number 8 in Tables 5 and 6 describes the pattern of trauma of a woman who was sexually abused between the ages of 7 and 12 and witnessed domestic violence when she was between the ages of 7 and 12. Studying these tables, one can begin to understand the severity of traumatization that many of the women experienced.

Table 3

Trauma Groups

Group	Number	Percentage of Participants	Score on Traumatic Antecedents Questionnaire
No Trauma	15	32%	0
Traumatized	15	32%	1,2
Highly Traumatized	9	19%	3,4
Severely Traumatized	8	17%	5 - 18

Table 4

Reports of Physical Abuse

School	Childhood	Latency	Adolescence
Psychology		1(2)	
Social Work	4(2),5,7,	4(2),5,6,7	4(2),5,6,7
Theology	16,17,18(2), 19,20,21,22	16,17,18(2) 19,20,21,22,23	17,18(3),23

Table 5

Reports of Sexual Abuse

School	Childhood	Latency	Adolescence
Psychology		2	
Social Work	4(2)	4(3),6,7, 8,9,10	6(6),4(7), 10,11,12
Theology	17,20,24,25(3)	17,22,23, 25(2),26	17,19,23,27,28(3),2 9,30

Table 6

Reports of Witnessing Domestic Violence

School	Childhood	Latency	Adolescence
Psychology		3	
Social Work	7,13	7,8(2),13,14,15	7,13
Theology	22,31	21,22,25,31	16,21,25,31

Note. Each number represents one of the women who reported trauma. Numbers in parentheses refer to violence by more than one perpetrator.

Ten women reported memories of being physically abused during childhood. Thirteen women (eight of whom reported earlier abuse during childhood) reported physical abuse during latency years. Seven (all of whom reported earlier abuse) reported physical abuse during adolescence. In all, 13 women reported being physically abused.

Five women reported being sexually abused before the age of seven. Twelve women (three of whom reported earlier sexual abuse) reported memories of sexual abuse between the ages of 7 and 12. Twelve women (five of whom reported earlier sexual abuse) reported sexual abuse between the ages of 13 and 18.

Four women described witnessing domestic violence before they were seven. Ten women (four of whom reported earlier memories of witnessing violence) described memories of witnessing domestic violence between the ages of 7 and

12. Six women (five of whom witnessed violence at younger ages) described witnessing domestic violence between the ages of 13 and 18.

Three women experienced both physical and sexual abuse. Two women experienced both physical abuse and witnessing domestic violence. One woman experienced sexual abuse and witnessed domestic violence. Two women experienced physical and sexual abuse and witnessed domestic violence.

Of the 15 psychology students I contacted to participate in the study, I interviewed 9 (not interviewing the other 6 because they had no known history of trauma). Three of the nine reported single types of abuse (one physical abuse during latency, one sexual abuse during latency, and one witnessing domestic violence during latency).

Of the 20 social work students I contacted, I interviewed 15 and did not interview 5 because they had histories of trauma, and many of the social work students I had already interviewed had histories of trauma. Of the 15 interviewed, 12 reported traumatic experiences. Five of these reported one type of trauma in one developmental stage. Three of these reported one type of trauma in more than one developmental stage. Three reported two types of trauma, with two of these in several developmental stages. One reported all three types of trauma at all three developmental stages.

Of the 25 theology students contacted, 23 were interviewed. Of these 23, 16 reported traumatic experiences. Six of these reported sexual abuse during one developmental stage. Two reported experiencing one type of trauma during all three developmental stages. Eight reported multiple types of trauma during several developmental stages.

In a random sample of nearly one thousand women in San Francisco, 38 percent of women reported one or more experiences of sexual abuse before the age of 18 (Russell, 1982). This compares with 53 percent of the social work students (8 of the 15 I interviewed) who reported sexual abuse; 11 percent of the psychology students (one of the nine I interviewed reported sexual abuse); and 52 percent of the theology students who reported sexual abuse (12 of the 23 I interviewed reported sexual abuse).[2]

---

[2]Frequency of trauma in the sample was compared with American studies on the frequency of physical and sexual abuse and domestic violence. Several participants grew up outside of the United States. While it was not possible to compare their experiences with national averages, Levinson's (1989) cross-cultural study of family violence in 90 societies highlights the prevalence of domestic violence (found in 84% of the 90 societies) and physical abuse of children (found in 74% of the 90 societies).

In the same national survey, 21 percent of the women interviewed report being physically abused by their spouses. We can compare this percentage with that of women who reported witnessing domestic violence when they were growing up. This compares with 33 percent of the social work students (5 of 15 reported witnessing domestic violence); 11 percent of the psychology students (1 of the 9 reported witnessing domestic violence) and 22 percent of the theology students (5 of the 23 reported witnessing domestic violence).

Finally, in a survey of over two thousand families conducted in 1975, Gelles and Straus (1988) found that 14 percent of the children suffered violence comparable to those surveyed in this study (that is, they were kicked, hit with a fist, hit with an object or beaten up). This compares with 27 percent of the social work students (4 of 15 reported physical abuse); 11 percent of the psychology students (1 out of 9 reported physical abuse), and 35 percent of the theology students (8 out of 23 reported physical abuse). The higher incidence of physical abuse in the present study, as compared with the 1975 survey, may be due in part to societal changes. When Gelles and Straus did a survey on family violence in 1985, they found that the rate for severe violence (being kicked, hit with a fist, hit with an object, or beaten up) dropped from 14 percent to 10.7 percent from 1975 to 1985. Gelles and Straus (1988) attribute this decline to growing public awareness of physical abuse. When we consider that the age range of women interviewed in the present study ranged from 21 to 58 years old, we might wonder whether the older the woman was, the higher the incidence of physical abuse in her generation.

In table 7, I compare percentages of physical abuse, sexual abuse and witnessing domestic violence derived from national surveys with percentages from the total sample of this study, and the percentages within the Schools of Theology and Social Work and the Department of Psychology. One might speculate from these figures that women studying social work have experienced more trauma, women studying theology have experienced as much trauma and women studying psychology have experienced less trauma than the average found in Russell's study. However, the present study may have attracted women from the Schools of Social Work and Theology who had been traumatized, and who wanted to explore their experiences, and may not have attracted women with similar experiences from the Department of Psychology.

What is important to acknowledge is that this sample has experienced slightly more trauma than an average sample of women. Taking into account the slight differences in percentages between the statistics collected in Russell's study, we may conclude that, on the whole, this sample is similar to a random sample of women, in terms of experiences of sexual violence, physical violence, and witnessing domestic violence.

Table 7

Comparison of Percentages of Trauma found in National Surveys and in this Sample

Type of Violence	National Studies	This Sample	Social Work	Psycho-logy	Theo-logy
Physical Abuse	14%	28%	27%	11%	35%
Sexual Abuse	38%	45%	53%	11%	52%
Witnessing Domestic Violence	21%	23%	33%	11%	22%

Note.
National Studies = Percentages found in Russell (1982) and Gelles and Straus (1988)
Total = Percentages in this sample
Social Work = Percentage of Social Work participants
Psychology = Percentage of Psychology participants
Theology = Percentage of Theology participants

Correlational Analyses of Traumatization and God Representations

The product moment correlation matrix for the 12 measures of God representations, the social desirability score, and the trauma score is presented in Table 8.

A positive relationship was hypothesized between wrathful God representations and traumatization. Scores for wrathful God representations on all scales (Metaphor, Adjective, and Adjusted Ranking Characterization of God Tasks) were positively, significantly correlated with traumatization (on the Wootton Metaphor Characterization of God Task $p < .05$, on the Adjective Characterization of God Task $p < .01$, and on the Wootton Adjusted Ranking Characterization of God Task $p < .01$) indicating that as traumatization increased, scores for wrathful God representations tended to increase.

A positive relationship was hypothesized between absent God representations and traumatization. Scores for absent God representations on two of the three scales (Adjective and Adjusted Ranking Characterization of God Tasks) were significantly positively correlated with traumatization ($p < .01$), indicating that as

Table 8

Correlational Matrix of God Representation Variables and Social Desirability with Traumatization Variable

	.MLG	.MOG	.MAG	.MMG	.ALG	.AOG	.AAG	.AMG	.RLG	.ROG	.RAG	.RWG	.SD
MLG	1.00												
MOG	-.13	1.00											
MAG	-.74**	-.26	1.00										
MMG	-.84**	-.05	.51**	1.00									
ALG	.76**	-.10	-.63**	-.62**	1.00								
AOG	.30*	.05	-.43**	-.18	.56**	1.00							
AAG	-.82**	-.17	.65**	.70**	-.75**	-.22	1.00						
AMG	-.45**	-.04	.07	.49**	-.23	.12	.51**	1.00					
RLG	.82**	-.07	-.61**	-.72**	.83**	.37*	-.77**	-.37*	1.00				
ROG	.24	.02	.02	.10	-.14	.16	-.14	-.38**	.19	1.00			
RAG	-.71**	-.00	.55**	.63**	-.74**	-.16	.79**	.33*	-.66**	-.05	1.00		
RWG	-.62**	.19	.21	.62**	-.49**	-.23	.45**	.67**	-.57**	-.29*	.40**	1.00	
SD	-.08	-.16	-.22	-.06	.18	-.14	-.16	-.06	.24	-.12	-.16	.03	1.00
TR	-.35*	-.14	.14	.32*	-.38**	-.21	.47**	.39**	-.49**	-.13	.48**	.41**	-.12

Note.
MLG, MOG, MAG, MMG: Loving, Observing, Absent, Wrathful God on the Metaphor Characterization of God Task
ALG, AOG, AAG, AMG: Loving, Observing, Absent, Wrathful God on the Adjective Characterization of God Task
RLG, ROG, RAG, RWG: Loving, Observing, Absent, Wrathful God on the Ranking Characterization of God Task
SD: Social Desirability
TR: Severity of Traumatization
Probability at a .01 level = .3721   ** $p < .01$
Probability at a .05 level = .2875   * $p < .05$

traumatization increased, scores on absent God representations tended to increase.

A negative relationship was hypothesized between loving God representations and traumatization. Scores for loving God representations on all of the three scales were significantly negatively correlated with traumatization (on the Wootton Metaphor Characterization of God Task $p < .05$, the Adjective Characterization of God Task $p < .01$, and the Wootton Adjusted Ranking Characterization of God Task $p < .01$), indicating that as traumatization increased, scores on loving God representations tended to decrease.

A negative relationship was hypothesized between observing God representations and traumatization. None of the scores for observing God representations on the three scales (Metaphor, Adjective and Ranking Characterization of God Tasks) were significantly correlated with traumatization, indicating little or no relationship between traumatization and scores on observing God representations.

Scores for social desirability were not significantly correlated with traumatization or God representations, indicating little or no relationship between social desirability and traumatization and social desirability and God representations.

Intercorrelations among God Representations

Convergent and discriminant validity of the God representation scales can be evaluated using the multitrait-multimethod program of analysis developed by Campbell and Fiske (1959). To accomplish this, the correlational matrix of all God Representation scales is used in the following four ways.

Heterotrait-Monomethod Triangles

Correlations among God representations can be used to consider the heterotrait-monomethod triangles on the correlational matrix, to address questions about the relationships between loving, observing, absent and wrathful God scales (the heterotraits) within each method (that is, the Metaphor, Adjective, and Ranking God Tasks). Discriminant validity can be demonstrated when the same pattern of trait relationships (that is, relationships between the different types of God representations) is the same across the three different methods of assessing God representations (Campbell & Fiske, 1959).

In the Wootton Metaphor Characterization of God Task, the loving God scale correlated negatively with both the absent and wrathful God scales, indicating that as loving God representations increased, absent and wrathful God representations tended to decrease. The absent God scale correlated positively with the wrathful God scale, indicating that as absent God representations increased, wrathful representations increased.

In the Adjective Characterization of God Task, there were significant positive correlations between the loving God and observing God scales, and between the absent God and wrathful God scales; and a negative correlation between loving God and absent God representations. As loving God representations increased, observing God representations tended to increase. As absent God representations increased, wrathful God representations tended to increase. As loving God representations increased, wrathful God representations tended to decrease.

In the Wootton Adjusted Ranking Characterization of God Task, the loving God scale correlated negatively with both the absent and wrathful God scales. As loving God representations increased, absent and wrathful God representations tended to decrease. The absent God scale correlated positively with the wrathful God scale, such that as absent God representations increased, wrathful representations tended to increase. On this scale there was also a negative correlation between observing God and wrathful God, indicating that as observing God representations increased, wrathful God representations tended to decrease. Table 9 summarizes these patterns of correlations.

It is clear that the two patterns that hold across all methods are the negative correlation between loving and absent God representations and the positive correlation between absent and wrathful God representations. A negative correlation between loving and wrathful God representations was a pattern for the Wootton Metaphor and Adjusted Ranking Characterization of God Tasks.

Table 9

Patterns of Correlations in Heterotrait Monomethod Triangles

God Representations	Loving	Observing	Absent	Wrathful
Loving				
Observing	AL+AO			
Absent	ML-MA AL-AA RL-RA			
Wrathful	ML-MW RL-RW	RO-RW	MA+MW AA+AW RA+RW	

Note.
ML, MO, MA, MW: The loving, observing, absent, wrathful God Representations on the Wootton Metaphor Characterization of God Task
AL, AO, AA, AW: The loving, observing, absent, wrathful God Representations on the Adjective Characterization of God Task
RL, RO, RA, RW: The loving, observing, absent, wrathful God Representations on the Wootton Adjusted Ranking Characterization of God Task
- : Negative Correlation
+ : Positive Correlation

Monotrait-Heteromethod Triangles

Correlations of the same scales (loving, observing, absent and wrathful) across different methods (Metaphor, Adjective, and Ranking Tasks) can also be compared to assess the validity of each scale. If these correlations are positive and significant, then this will demonstrate the validity of the scales.

The correlations between loving God representations across all three God representation tasks were positively correlated. The correlations between observing God representations were not significantly correlated among any of the three God representation tasks. The correlations between absent God representations across all three God representation tasks were positively correlated. The correlations between wrathful God representations across all three God representation tasks were positively correlated. Table 10 summarizes these patterns of correlations, which demonstrate the convergent validity of the loving, absent and wrathful God scales, but not the observing God scales.

Table 10

Patterns of Correlations in Monotrait Heteromethod Triangles

God Rep.	Loving	Observing	Absent	Wrathful
Loving	ML+AL ML+RL AL+RL			
Observing				
Absent			MA+AA MA+RA AA+RA	
Wrathful				MW+AW MW+RW AW+RW

Note.
ML, MO, MA, MW: The loving, observing, absent, wrathful God Representations on the Wootton Metaphor Characterization of God Task
AL, AO, AA, AW: The loving, observing, absent, wrathful God Representations on the Adjective Characterization of God Task
RL, RO, RA, RW: The loving, observing, absent, wrathful God Representations on the Wootton Adjusted Ranking Characterization of God Task
- : Negative Correlation
+ : Positive Correlation

Monotrait Correlations Compared with Monomethod Correlations

Correlations among God representations can be compared to see whether the correlation of a particular scale (for example, loving God representation) between methods (for example, Metaphor loving God and Adjective loving God) is higher than correlations among one method (in this case, the correlations between loving, observing, absent and wrathful God correlations within the Wootton Metaphor Characterization of God Task.) It makes sense that if each characterization of God task is measuring the same internal God representation then correlations between the same representations on different tasks should be higher than correlations (positive or negative) between different God representations.

Tables 11 to 13 below make all these comparisons. For at least two thirds of these comparisons, monotrait correlations (correlations between the same scale across methods) were higher than correlations between different scales within the same methods. Monotrait correlations between loving God scales were higher for 15 of the 18 correlations between loving God and other God representations. Monotrait correlations between wrathful God scales were higher for 12 of the 18 correlations between the wrathful God and other God representations. Monotrait correlations between absent God scales were higher than 11 of the 18 correlations between the absent God and other God representations. This further demonstrates the validity of the loving, absent and wrathful God scales.

Table 11

Monotrait Correlations Compared with Monomethod Correlations: Loving God Representations

	MONO-	METHOD				
MONO-TRAIT	ML-MA -.74	ML-MW -.84	AL+AO .56	AL+AA .75	RL-RW -.57	RL-RA -.66
ML+AL .76	>	<	>	>	>	>
ML+RL .82	>	<	>	>	>	>
AL+RL .83	>	<	>	>	>	>

Note.
ML, MO, MA, MW: The loving, observing, absent, wrathful God Representations on the Wootton Metaphor Characterization of God Task
AL, AO, AA, AW: The loving, observing, absent, wrathful God Representations on the Adjective Characterization of God Task
RL, RO, RA, RW: The loving, observing, absent, wrathful God Representations on the Wootton Adjusted Ranking Characterization of God Task
< : the correlation in the row is less than the correlation in the column.
> : the correlation in the row is greater than the correlation in the column

Table 12

Monotrait Correlations Compared with Monomethod Correlations: Wrathful God Representations

	MONO-	METHOD				
MONO-TRAIT	MW-ML -.84	MW+MA .51	AW+AA .51	RW-RL -.57	RW-RO -.29	RW*RW .40
MW+AW .49	<	.<	<	<	>	>
MW+RW .62	<	>	>	>	>	>
AW+RW .67	<	>	>	>	>	>

Note.

ML, MO, MA, MW: The loving, observing, absent, wrathful God Representations on the Wootton Metaphor Characterization of God Task

AL, AO, AA, AW: The loving, observing, absent, wrathful God Representations on the Adjective Characterization of God Task

RL, RO, RA, RW: The loving, observing, absent, wrathful God Representations on the Wootton Adjusted Ranking Characterization of God Task

< : the correlation in the row is less than the correlation in the column.
> : the correlation in the row is greater than the correlation in the column

Table 13

Monotrait Correlations Compared with Monomethod Correlations: Absent God Representations

	MONO-	METHOD				
MONO-TRAIT	MA+MW .51	MA-ML -.74	AA+AW .51	AA-AL -.75	RA+RW .40	RA-RL -.66
MA+AA .64	>	<	>	<	>	<
MA+RA .55	>	<	>	<	>	<
AA+AR .79	>	>	>	>	>	>

Note.

ML, MO, MA, MW: The loving, observing, absent, wrathful God Representations on the Wootton Metaphor Characterization of God Task

AL, AO, AA, AW: The loving, observing, absent, wrathful God Representations on the Adjective Characterization of God Task

RL, RO, RA, RW: The loving, observing, absent, wrathful God Representations on the Wootton Adjusted Ranking Characterization of God Task

< : the correlation in the row is less than the correlation in the column.

> : the correlation in the row is greater than the correlation in the column.

Patterns of Scale Interrelationships

A final comparison which can be made among the God representation correlations concerns the patterns of scale inter-relationships, both within and across methods. All possible pairs of correlations involving the loving God and wrathful God scales were significant and in the expected direction, with one exception. All wrathful God scales correlated significantly with all other wrathful God scales and negatively and significantly with all loving God scales, both within and across methods. The only exception was the correlation between loving and wrathful God scales on the Adjective Characterization of God Task. Table 14 highlights these patterns of significant correlations.

All possible pairs of correlations involving the loving God and absent God scales were in the expected direction and significant (see Table 15). All absent God scales correlated significantly with all other absent God scales and negatively and significantly with all loving God scales, both within and across methods.

All possible pairs of correlations involving the absent God and wrathful God scales were in the expected direction and significant (Table 16). All absent God scales correlated significantly with all other absent God scales and positively and significantly with all wrathful God scales, both within and across methods, with two exceptions (the correlations between the absent God Scale on the WMCGT and the wrathful God Scales on both the ACGT and WARCGT).

Table 14

Pairs of Correlations involving Loving and Wrathful God Scales

	ML	AL	RL	MW	AW	RW
ML	1.00					
AL	.76	1.00				
RL	.82	.83	1.00			
MW	-.84	-.62	-.72	1.00		
AW	-.45	ns	-.37	.49	1.00	
RW	-.61	-.49	-.57	.62	.67	1.00

Table 15

Pairs of Correlations involving Loving and Absent God Scales

	ML	AL	RL	MA	AA	RA
ML	1.00					
AL	.76	1.00				
RL	.82	.83	1.00			
MA	-.74	-.63	-.61	1.00		
AA	-.82	-.75	-.77	.64	1.00	
RA	-.71	-.74	-.66	.55	.79	1.00

Note.
ML, MO, MA, MW: The loving, observing, absent, wrathful God Representations on the Wootton Metaphor Characterization of God Task
AL, AO, AA, AW: The loving, observing, absent, wrathful God Representations on the Adjective Characterization of God Task
RL, RO, RA, RW: The loving, observing, absent, wrathful God Representations on the Wootton Adjusted Ranking Characterization of God Task

Table 16

Pairs of Correlations involving Absent and Wrathful God Scales

	MA	AA	RA	MW	AW	RW
MA	1.00					
AA	.64	1.00				
RA	.55	.79	1.00			
MW	.51	.70	.63	1.00		
AW	ns	.51	.33	.49	1.00	
RW	ns	.45	.40	.62	.67	1.00

Note.
ML, MO, MA, MW: The loving, observing, absent, wrathful God
Representations on the Wootton Metaphor Characterization of God Task
AL, AO, AA, AW: The loving, observing, absent, wrathful God Representations
on the Adjective Characterization of God Task
RL, RO, RA, RW: The loving, observing, absent, wrathful God Representations
on the Wootton Adjusted Ranking Characterization of God Task

The correlations with observing God scales were not compared because only
3 out of a possible 30 correlations were significant.

We may conclude that the loving, wrathful and absent God scales are
assessing the same constructs (with there being some possible overlap between the
absent and wrathful God scales). Items on all the observing God scales do not
describe one construct. The significance of these findings will be considered more
fully in the next chapter. It may be noted at this point, however, that overall, the
multitrait-multimethod analysis demonstrates the validity of three of the four
scales: the loving, absent and wrathful God scales.

Correlations with Social Desirability

None of the 12 God representations was significantly correlated with scores
on the Marlowe-Crowne Social Desirability Scale, indicating that the way
participants described God was not significantly influenced by a desire to appear
in a favorable light. As well, the social desirability scores were not significantly
correlated with severity of traumatization, indicating that severity of

traumatization scores were not influenced by a desire to appear in a favorable light.

We might suppose that graduate students in a School of Theology, many of whom are or will be religious professionals, might be concerned with appearing in a favorable light. They might try to present their images of God in a way that is socially desirable. However, School of Theology students were no different from Social Work or Psychology students, in that none of these groups showed a significant correlation between social desirability scores and God representation scores. This was further demonstrated in a multiple regression analyzing the covariance of God representations and social desirability with traumatization. The covariance of social desirability was demonstrated to be very low (see next section).

Multiple Regressions: Traumatization and God Representations

Standard multiple regression analyses (Tabachnick & Fidell, 1983, p. 101) were carried out, using traumatization as the criterion variable and God representations as predictor variables. These analyses indicated how much of the variance of Trauma scores was associated with multiple God representations and how much of unique variance was contributed by each God representation. Social desirability scores were not entered in these analyses, because they were not significantly correlated with trauma or God representations and because correlations between trauma and God representations remained virtually unchanged when covariance with social desirability was eliminated by partial correlation, as shown in Table 17.

The Covariance of All God Representation Scales

A multiple regression analysis of traumatization and God representations can be used to assess the unique contribution of each God representation towards predicting scores on traumatization. In Table 18, when each partial r squared value is multiplied by 100, this gives the percentage of prediction uniquely contributed by a God representation. For example, the loving God representation on the Adjective Characterization God Task (AL) has a partial r squared of .0903, and this particular scale uniquely contributes 9 percent towards the overall prediction of scores on traumatization using God representations. In Table 18, the percentage value in the last column describes percentage of the unique contribution of each God representation to the overall correlation between traumatization and God representations.

Table 17

Changes in Correlations between Trauma Scores and God Representation Scores when Co-variance with Social Desirability Scores has been Eliminated by Partial Correlation

God Representation	Simple Correlation	Partial Correlation
Metaphor: Loving God	-.3492	-.3433
Observing God	.1394	.1616
Absent God	.1389	.1164
Wrathful God	.3177	.3137
Adjective: Loving God	-.3809	-.3677
Observing God	-.2077	-.2283
Absent God	.4702	.4603
Wrathful God	.3929	.3890
Ranking: Loving God	-.4931	-.4817
Observing God	-.1340	-.1501
Absent God	.4819	.4720
Wrathful God	.4142	.4208

Table 18

The Covariance of each God Representation

God Representations	Simple r sq.	Partial r sq.	% of var.
Metaphor: Loving God	.1219	.0046	.4%
Observing God	.0194	.0055	.5%
Absent God	.0193	.0097	.9%
Wrathful God	.1009	.0077	.7%
Adjective: Loving God	.1451	.0903	9%
Observing God	.0432	.0693	7%
Absent God	.2211	.0246	2%
Wrathful God	.1543	.0070	.7%
Ranking: Loving God	.2432	.1513	15%
Observing God	.0180	.0014	.1%
Absent God	.2322	.1289	12%
Wrathful God	.1715	.0118	1%

The multiple correlation between traumatization and the 12 God representations was .70, which accounted for 49 percent (R squared) of the variance of Trauma scores. The unique contribution of each God representation to the variance of Trauma scores was relatively low, with only the loving God and absent God representations on the ranking scale (RL and RA) contributing more than 10 percent. The low unique contributions occurred because the correlations among many predictor variables were high (see Table 8). If the predictor variables had not been correlated, unique contributions would tend to be higher.

The Covariance of God Representations for each Method

The results of separate multiple regressions for each God Representation method (Metaphor, Adjective, Ranking) are shown in the following tables (Tables 19, 20, and 21).

Table 19

Multiple Regressions for the Wootton Metaphor Characterization of God Task

God Representation	Simple r sq.	Partial r sq.	% of Var.
Loving God	.1219	.0118	1%
Observing God	.0194	.0081	.8%
Absent God	.0193	.0116	1%
Wrathful God	.1009	.0083	.8%

Table 20

Multiple Regressions for the Adjective Characterization of God Task

God Representation	Simple r sq.	Partial r sq.	% of Var.
Loving God	.1451	.0000	0%
Observing God	.0432	.0229	2%
Absent God	.2211	.0349	3%
Wrathful God	.1543	.0603	6%

Table 21

Multiple Regressions for the Wootton Adjusted Ranking Characterization of God Task

God Representation	Simple r sq.	Partial r sq.	% of Var.
Loving God	.2432	.0269	2%
Observing God	.0180	.0011	.1%
Absent God	.2322	.0578	6%
Wrathful God	.1715	.0286	3%

For the Metaphor scale (Table 19), only 16 percent of the variance of Trauma is accounted for by the four God representations and none of the God representations contributes as much as 2 percent unique variance. For the

Adjective scale (Table 20), the four God representations account for 28 percent of the variance of Trauma scores, and the only large unique contribution is 6 percent from the wrathful God representations. For the Ranking scale (Table 21), the four God representations account for 31 percent of the variance of Trauma scores and only absent God representations contribute as much as 6 percent unique variance.

Once again, the unique contribution of each God representation is limited by the high intercorrelations among three of the four predictor variables. These three variables (loving, absent and wrathful God) were substantially correlated with Trauma scores for the most part, as indicated by the simple r squared covariances in Tables 19, 20 and 21, but were highly correlated with each other (Table 8). The only exception to this was the absent God scale on the <u>Wootton Metaphor Characterization of God Task</u>. The remaining variable (observing God) was not highly correlated with Trauma scores and thus could not make a large unique contribution.

Analyses of Variance: Traumatization and God Representations

As another way of assessing the effect of trauma on reports of God representations, participants were divided into groups in terms of Trauma score. As was noted earlier, this decision to subdivide the sample into Trauma groups was made after the correlational analyses were done. Since the correlation was non linear, a repeated measures analysis of variance was a way to further explore the relationship between degree of traumatization and God representations.

The No Traumatization group included 15 participants with Trauma scores of 0, the Traumatized group included 15 participants with Trauma scores of 1 or 2, the Highly Traumatized group included 9 participants with Trauma scores of 3 and 4, and the Severely Traumatized group included 8 participants with Trauma scores of 5 to 18.

Analyses of variance were carried out in which Groups was one independent variable with four levels of trauma, and God representations was a repeated measurement independent variable with four levels (loving, observing, absent, and wrathful God). The dependent variable was the God representation score. The analysis of variance was a four by four factorial design with two main effects (Groups and God representations) and one interaction (Groups times God representations). A separate analysis was carried out for each of the God representation scales.

Metaphor Scale

The results for the Metaphor Scale were used in the first analysis. The means on each Metaphor Scale in each Trauma group are shown in Table 22. The main effect for Trauma Groups was not significant, with the overall means for the four groups being almost identical. The main effect for God representations was highly significant ($p < .001$), with large differences in mean scores between the four God representations.

Of most interest to the present study was the interaction between Groups and God representations, which was highly significant ($p < .0001$). As shown in Table 22 and Figure 1, the mean God representations for the Not Traumatized, Traumatized, and Highly Traumatized groups were very similar, but the Severely Traumatized group had lower loving God representations and higher absent and wrathful God representations.

Further statistical analysis of the significant interaction by the Fisher LSD post hoc test, using $p < .05$ and $p < .01$ as the level of significance, showed that

1. the Severely Traumatized group scored significantly lower ($p < .01$) than the other three groups on loving God representations;
2. the Severely Traumatized group scored significantly higher ($p < .05$) than the Traumatized and Highly Traumatized groups on observant God representations;
3. the Severely Traumatized group scored significantly higher ($p < .05$) than the Not Traumatized group on absent God representations;
4. the Severely Traumatized group scored significantly higher than the Not Traumatized Group ($p < .01$) and the Traumatized Group ($p < .05$).

The results of the repeated measures analysis of variance demonstrate that on the Wootton Metaphor Characterization of God Task, there is no significant correlation between severity of traumatization and God representations, until traumatization is severe.

Table 22

Means on Each Metaphor Scale in each Trauma Group

God Representation	Trauma Groups	Mean
Loving God	Not Traumatized	80.6
	Traumatized	82.13
	Highly Traumatized	78.44
	Severely Traumatized	60.87
Observing God	Not Traumatized	65.53
	Traumatized	60.13
	Highly Traumatized	60.11
	Severely Traumatized	66.62
Absent God	Not Traumatized	54.13
	Traumatized	56.27
	Highly Traumatized	57.33
	Severely Traumatized	61.
Wrathful God	Not Traumatized	39.73
	Traumatized	41.47
	Highly Traumatized	43.78
	Severely Traumatized	51.37

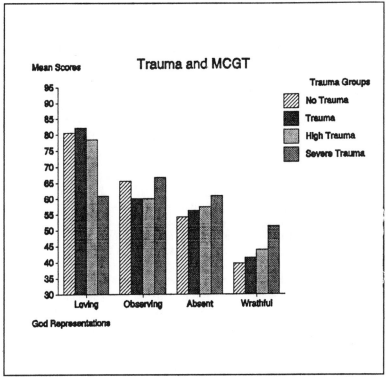

Figure 1. Comparison of Metaphor God Representation Scores among Trauma
Groups.

Table 23

Trauma Groups and Metaphor Scales: F Ratio and Probability of Repeated
ANOVA

Source of Variance	F-Ratio	Probability
Trauma Groups (TG)	1.27	.2976
God Representations (GR)	87.56	.0000
Interaction (TG and GR)	4.19	.0001

Adjective Scale

The results for the Adjective Scale were analyzed next. The means on each ACGT scale in each Trauma group are shown in Table 24. Once again the main effect for Groups was not significant and the main effect for God representations and the interaction were highly significant ($p < .001$) (Table 25). The results for the Not Traumatized, Traumatized, and Highly Traumatized groups were very similar, but the Severely Traumatized group had lower loving God representations and higher absent and wrathful God representations (Figure 2). Statistical analysis by the Fisher LSD post hoc test showed that

1. the Severely Traumatized group scored significantly lower than the other three groups on loving God representations ($p < .01$ for Not Traumatized and Traumatized; $p < .05$ for Highly Traumatized);
2. the Severely Traumatized group scored significantly lower ($pp < .05$) than the Not Traumatized group on observant God representations;
3. the Severely Traumatized group scored significantly higher ($p < .01$) than the other three groups on absent God representations;
4. the Severely Traumatized group scored significantly higher than the other three groups on wrathful God representations ($p < .01$ for Highly Traumatized; $p < .05$ for Not Traumatized and Traumatized).

The results of the repeated measures analysis of variance demonstrate that on the Adjective Characterization of God Task, there is no significant correlation between severity of traumatization and God representations, until traumatization is severe.

Table 24

Means on Each Adjective Scale in each Trauma Group

God Representation	Trauma Groups	Mean
Loving God	Not Traumatized	50.47
	Traumatized	49.4
	Highly Traumatized	48.11
	Severely Traumatized	35.75
Observing God	Not Traumatized	42.67
	Traumatized	39.13
	Highly Traumatized	38.44
	Severely Traumatized	37.25
Absent God	Not Traumatized	24.07
	Traumatized	24.93
	Highly Traumatized	27.89
	Severely Traumatized	40.5
Wrathful God	Not Traumatized	28.27
	Traumatized	28.6
	Highly Traumatized	26.33
	Severely Traumatized	37

Table 25

Trauma Groups and Adjective Scales: F Ratio and Probability of Repeated ANOVA

Source of Variance	F-Ratio	Probability
Trauma Groups (TG)	0.63	.5970
God Representations (GR)	55.46	.0000
Interaction (TG and GR)	5.65	.0000

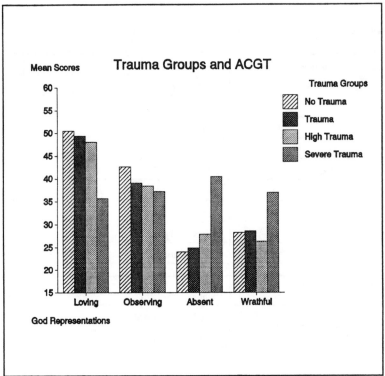

<u>Figure 2</u>. Comparison of Adjective God Representation Scores among Trauma Groups.

Ranking Scale

The results for the Ranking Scale were similar to those for the other scales, as shown in Tables 26 and 27 and Figure 3. The main effect for Trauma Groups (Table 27) was not significant, but the main effect for God representations and the interaction were highly significant ($p < .001$). Using the $p < .01$ significance criterion, the Severe group scored significantly lower in loving God representations and significantly higher in absent God and wrathful God representations.

Table 26

Means on Each Ranking Scale in each Trauma Group

God Representation	Trauma Groups	Mean
Loving God	Not Traumatized	7.87
	Traumatized	7.73
	Highly Traumatized	8
	Severely Traumatized	3.37
Observing God	Not Traumatized	6.27
	Traumatized	6.07
	Highly Traumatized	6.44
	Severely Traumatized	5.75
Absent God	Not Traumatized	2.6
	Traumatized	3
	Highly Traumatized	2.89
	Severely Traumatized	7
Wrathful God	Not Traumatized	2
	Traumatized	1.8
	Highly Traumatized	2
	Severely Traumatized	4.62

Table 27

Trauma Groups and Ranking Scales: F Ratio and Probability

Source of Variance	F-Ratio	Probability
Trauma Groups (TG)	0.69	.5645
God Representations (GR)	32.35	.0000
Interaction (TG and GR)	4.66	.0000

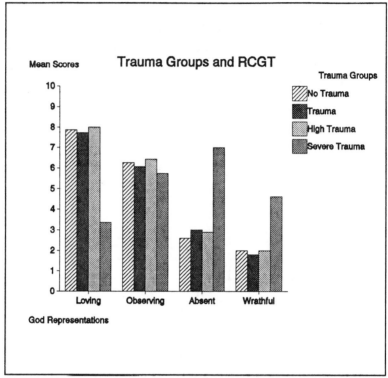

Figure 3. Comparison of Ranking God Representation Scores among Trauma Groups.

As Figure 3 shows, the results for the Not Traumatized, Traumatized, Highly Traumatized groups were very similar, but the Severely Traumatized group had lower loving God representations and higher absent and wrathful God representations. Statistical analysis by the Fisher LSD post hoc test showed that

1. the Severely Traumatized group scored significantly lower than the other three groups on loving God representations ($p < .01$);
2. the Severely Traumatized group scored significantly higher ($p < .01$) than the other three groups on absent God representations;
3. the Severely Traumatized group scored significantly higher than the other three groups on wrathful God representations ($p < .05$).

The results of the repeated measures analysis of variance demonstrate that on the Wootton Adjusted Ranking Characterization of God Task, there is no significant correlation between severity of traumatization and God representations, until traumatization is severe.

Summary

The results obtained for the three scales were remarkably similar, showing strong convergent evidence that no traumatization, traumatization, and high traumatization as defined by the present groupings were not correlated with God representation scores, whereas severe traumatization was significantly correlated with lower loving God scores and higher absent God and wrathful God scores. Only the observing God scores were not correlated with severe trauma.

Initial correlational analyses demonstrated significant negative correlations between degree of traumatization and loving God representations, significant positive correlations between degree of traumatization and absent and wrathful God representations, and no significant correlations between degree of traumatization and observant God representations. The repeated measures analysis of variance demonstrates that these correlations are only significant for the severely traumatized group, and that there is no significant correlation between severity of traumatization and God representations for the first three groups: no trauma, trauma and high trauma.

Additional Analyses

Additional statistical analyses of the relationship between traumatization and self report on trauma, alcoholic parents, ethnicity and childhood religion were carried out. The analysis of the relationship between traumatization and self report was part of the experimental design but the other analyses were not pre-planned as part of the formal experimental design. They must be considered exploratory and suggestive rather than definitive.

Traumatization and Self Report

A correlational analysis of the relationship between the scores on the simple self report on severity of traumatization and the severity of traumatization scale was undertaken. This indicated how effective the simple self report was in screening participants. The correlation between scores on the Traumatic Antecedents Questionnaire and the screening question was .65 ($p > .01$). While this indicated a significant correlation, it accounted for only 42 percent of the variance of the trauma questionnaire, and was not adequate as a substitute for the Traumatic Antecedents Questionnaire in assessing severity of traumatization.

Alcoholic Parents, Trauma, and God Representations

A correlational analysis of the relationship between scores on traumatization and alcoholism was done. The correlation (.42) was positively significant ($p < .01$), indicating that as traumatization increased, the probability of one parent or both being alcoholic tended to increase.

Correlations between the presence of an alcoholic parent and God representation scores was further explored using a repeated measures ANOVA, comparing the mean scores on each God representation scale for those who described her parent or parents as alcoholic (there were 17 participants in Group 2) and those who did not (there were 30 participants in Group 1). The results of this analysis are shown in Tables 28 and 29.

Table 28

Means on Each Metaphor Scale in each Parent Group

God Representations	Parent Groups	Mean
Loving God	No Alcoholism	80.33
	Alcoholism	72
Observing God	No Alcoholism	64.23
	Alcoholism	60.71
Absent God	No Alcoholism	55.03
	Alcoholism	59.35
Wrathful God	No Alcoholism	40.3
	Alcoholism	47.88

Table 29

Parent Groups and Metaphor Scales: F Ratio and Probability of Repeated ANOVA

Source	F-Ratio	Probability
Parent Groups (PG)	.09	.7708
God Representations (GR)	78.33	.0000
Interaction (PG and GR)	4.70	.0037

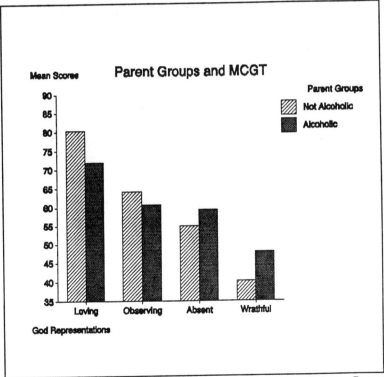

Figure 4. Comparison of Metaphor God Representation Scores between Parent Groups.

As Figure 4 illustrates, the group who had an alcoholic parent had lower loving God representations and higher absent and wrathful God representations. Statistical analysis by the Fisher LSD post hoc test showed that

1. the Alcoholic Parent group scored significantly lower on loving God representations ($p < .05$);
2. the Alcoholic Parent group scored significantly higher ($p < .05$) on absent God representations;
3. the Alcoholic Parent group scored significantly higher on wrathful God representations ($p < .05$).

The same repeated ANOVA was done with the Adjective Characterization of God Task. The mean God representation score for each group is shown in Table 30, and the probability of the interaction is shown in Table 31.

Table 30

Means on Each Adjective Scale in Each Parent Group

God Representations	Parent Groups	Mean
Loving God	No Alcoholism	50.7
	Alcoholism	40.94
Observing God	No Alcoholism	41.4
	Alcoholism	37
Absent God	No Alcoholism	25.37
	Alcoholism	32.29
Wrathful God	No Alcoholism	28.67
	Alcoholism	30.94

Table 31

Parent Groups and Adjective Scales: F Ratio and Probability of Repeated ANOVA

Source	F-Ratio	Probability
Parent Groups (PG)	1.01	.3201
God Representations (GR)	48.38	.0000
Interaction (PG and GR)	7.29	.0001

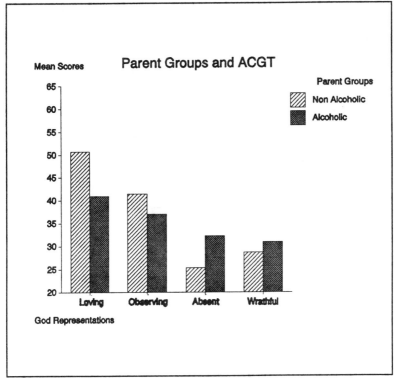

Figure 5. Comparison of Adjective God Representation Scores between Parent Groups.

As Figure 5 illustrates, those who reported having an alcoholic parent have lower mean scores for the loving and observing God scales and a higher mean score on the absent God scale. Statistical analysis by the Fisher LSD post hoc test showed that

1. the Alcoholic Parent group scored significantly lower on loving God representations ($p < .01$);
2. The Alcoholic Parent group scored significantly lower on observing God representations ($p < .01$);
3. the Alcoholic Parent group scored significantly higher ($p < .05$) on absent God representations.

Finally, the same repeated ANOVA was done with the Wootton Adjusted Ranking Characterization of God Task. The mean God representation score for each group is shown in Table 32 and the probability of the interaction is shown in Table 33.

Table 32

Means on Each Ranking Scale in Each Parent Group

God Representations	Parent Groups	Mean
Loving God	No Alcoholism	7.9
	Alcoholism	5.65
Observing God	No Alcoholism	6.13
	Alcoholism	6.18
Absent God	No Alcoholism	2.6
	Alcoholism	5.18
Wrathful God	No Alcoholism	1.83
	Alcoholism	3.35

Table 33

Parent Groups and Ranking Scales: F Ratio and Probability of Repeated ANOVA

Source	F-Ratio	Probability
Parent Groups (PG)	3.04	.0880
God Representations (GR)	28.98	.0000
Interaction (PG and GR)	6.07	.0007

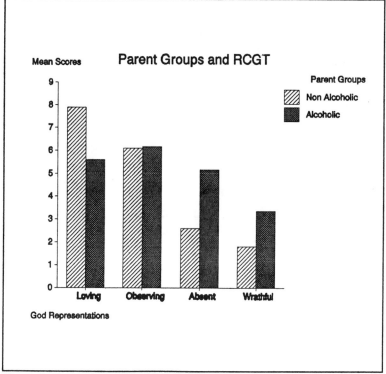

Figure 6. Comparison of Ranking God Representation Scores between Parent Groups.

As Figure 6 illustrates, those who reported having an alcoholic parent have lower mean scores on the loving God scale and a higher mean score on the absent God scale. Statistical analysis by the Fisher LSD post hoc test showed that

1. the Alcoholic Parent group scored significantly lower on loving God representations ($p < .05$);
2. the Alcoholic Parent group scored significantly higher ($p < .05$) on absent God representations.

Ethnicity and God Representations

Correlations between Caucasian-nonCaucasian groups and God representation scores were explored using a repeated measures ANOVA, comparing the mean scores on each God representation scale for those who were Black, Hispanic or Asian (there were 7 participants in Group 2) and those who were Caucasian (there were 40 participants in Group 1).

The results of the repeated measures ANOVA comparing mean scores on the Metaphor scales are shown in Tables 34 and 35.

Table 34

Means on Each Metaphor Scale in Each Ethnic Group

God Representations	Ethnic Groups	Mean
Loving God	Caucasian	79.7
	Black, Hispanic, Asian	63.71
Observing God	Caucasian	62.25
	Black, Hispanic, Asian	67
Absent God	Caucasian	56.62
	Black, Hispanic, Asian	56.43
Wrathful God	Caucasian	41.32
	Black, Hispanic, Asian	52.86

Table 35

Ethnic Groups and Metaphor Scales: F Ratio and Probability of Repeated ANOVA

Source	F-Ratio	Probability
Ethnic Groups (EG)	.28	.5998
God Representations (GR)	82.00	.0000
Interaction (EG and GR)	7.03	.0002

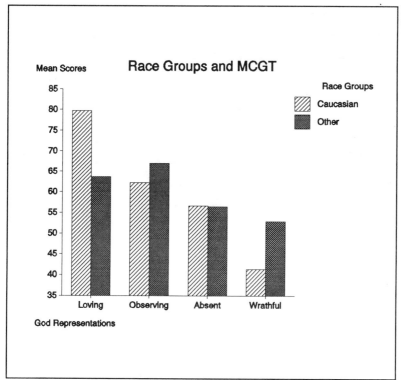

Figure 7. Comparison of Metaphor God Representation Scores between Ethnic Groups.

As Figure 7 illustrates, those who were Black, Hispanic or Asian had a significantly lower mean score ($p < .01$) for loving God and a higher mean scores ($p < .01$) for wrathful God (this was determined by using a Fisher LSD post hoc test).

The same repeated ANOVA was done with the Adjective Characterization of God Task. The mean God representation score for each group is shown in Table 36 and the probability of the interaction is shown in Table 37.

Table 36

Means on Each Adjective Scale in Each Ethnic Group

God Representations	Ethnic Groups	Mean
Loving God	Caucasian	50.7
	Black, Hispanic, Asian	42.14
Observing God	Caucasian	48.05
	Black, Hispanic, Asian	42
Absent God	Caucasian	26.7
	Black, Hispanic, Asian	34.57
Wrathful God	Caucasian	27.75
	Black, Hispanic, Asian	39.43

Table 37

Ethnic Groups and Adjective Scales: F Ratio and Probability of Repeated ANOVA

Source	F-Ratio	Probability
Ethnic Groups (EG)	6.67	.0131
God Representations (GR)	45.38	.0000
Interaction (EG and GR)	4.04	.0087

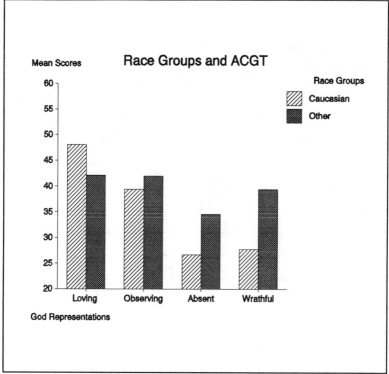

Figure 8. Comparison of Adjective God Representation Scores between Ethnic Groups.

As Figure 8 illustrates, those who are Black, Asian and Hispanic had a significantly higher mean score ($p < .01$) on the wrathful God scale (this was determined by using a Fisher LSD post hoc test).

Finally, the same repeated ANOVA was done with the Wootton Adjusted Ranking Characterization of God Task. The mean God representation score for each group is shown in Table 38 and the probability of the interaction is shown in Table 39.

Table 38

Means on Each Ranking Scale in Each Ethnic Group

God Representations	Ethnic Groups	Mean
Loving God	Caucasian	7.27
	Black, Hispanic, Asian	6
Observing God	Caucasian	6.25
	Black, Hispanic, Asian	5.57
Absent God	Caucasian	3.2
	Black, Hispanic, Asian	5.43
Wrathful God	Caucasian	1.82
	Black, Hispanic, Asian	5.57

Table 39

Ethnic Groups and Ranking Scales: F Ratio and Probability of Repeated ANOVA

Source	F-Ratio	Probability
Ethnic Groups (EG)	8.44	.0057
God Representations (GR)	27.90	.0000
Interaction (EG and GR)	4.16	.0074

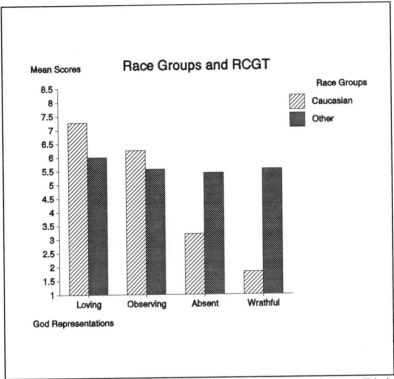

Figure 9. Comparison of Ranking God Representation Scores between Ethnic Groups.

As Figure 9 illustrates, those who were Black, Asian or Hispanic have a significantly higher mean score ($p < .01$) on the wrathful God scale (this was determined using a Fisher LSD post hoc test).

Role of Childhood Religion and God Representations

In the final repeated analysis of variance, I considered the relationship between the role of childhood religion and God representation scores. Tables 40 to 45 and Figures 10 to 12 show the results of these analyses.

Table 40

Means on Each Metaphor Scale in Each Childhood Religion Group

God Representation	Role of Religion in Childhood	Mean
Loving God	Minor	75
	Major Positive	83.04
	Major Negative	71.56
	Major Positive & Negative	67.75
Observing God	Minor	62.15
	Major Positive	63.62
	Major Negative	61.11
	Major Negative & Positive	66.25
Absent God	Minor	57.15
	Major Positive	53.95
	Major Negative	61.66
	Major Negative & Positive	57.25
Wrathful God	Minor	45.69
	Major Positive	39.24
	Major Negative	45.55
	Major Negative & Positive	48.75

Table 41

Childhood Religion Groups and Metaphor Scales: F Ratio and Probability of Repeated ANOVA

Source of Variance	F-Ratio	Probability
Role of Religion in Childhood (RRC)	0.30	.8238
God Representations (GR)	78.52	.0000
Interaction (RRC and GR)	2.27	.0212

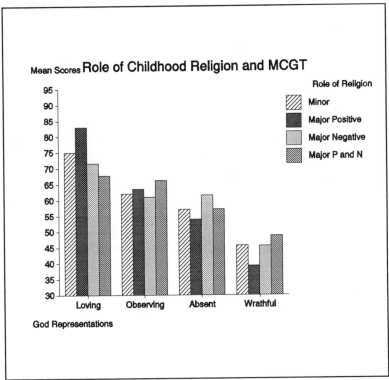

Figure 10. Comparison of Metaphor God Representation Scores among Childhood Religion Groups.

Figure 10 shows the differences between mean scores for the childhood religion groups. On the Metaphor Loving God Scale, those who said that religion played a major positive role had significantly higher scores than those who described religion as playing a major negative, and major positive and negative role in childhood ($p < .05$). On the Metaphor Absent God Scale, those who described religion as playing a major positive role had a significantly lower score from those who described religion as playing a major negative role ($p < .01$). These significant differences were determined using a Fisher LSD post hoc test.

Table 42

Means on Each Adjective Scale in Each Childhood Religion Group

God Representation	Role of Religion in Childhood	Mean
Loving God	Minor	43.77
	Major Positive	52.38
	Major Negative	42.44
	Major Positive & Negative	41.5
Observing God	Minor	39.69
	Major Positive	40.19
	Major Negative	39.67
	Major Negative & Positive	38.5
Absent God	Minor	27.46
	Major Positive	23.86
	Major Negative	34.56
	Major Negative & Positive	35.25
Wrathful God	Minor	27.31
	Major Positive	28.33
	Major Negative	30.89
	Major Negative & Positive	39.5

Table 43

Childhood Religion Groups and Adjective Scales: F Ratio and Probability of Repeated ANOVA

Source of Variance	F-Ratio	Probability
Role of Religion in Childhood (RRC)	1.31	.2839
God Representations (GR)	48.57	.0000
Interaction (RRC and GR)	3.16	.0017

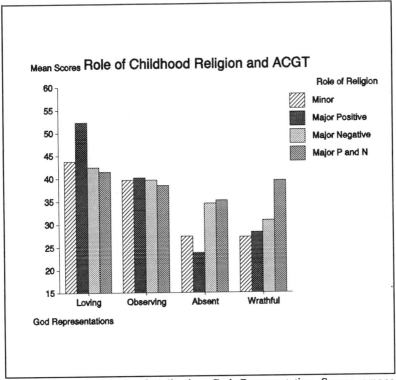

Figure 11. Comparison of Adjective God Representation Scores among Childhood Religion Groups.

As Figure 11 shows, those who described religion as playing a major positive role in their childhood had a significantly higher Adjective Loving God score than those who described religion as playing a minor role in childhood ($p < .05$), and those who described religion as playing a major negative role and a major positive and negative in childhood ($p < .01$). On the Adjective Absent God scale, the group who described the role of religion in childhood as major positive had a significantly lower score than those who described religion as playing a major negative role and those who described religion as playing a major negative and positive role in childhood ($p < .01$). On the Adjective Wrathful God scale, the group who described religion as playing a major negative and positive role in childhood had a significantly higher score than those who described religion as playing a minor role in childhood ($p < .01$) and those who described religion as playing a major positive role in childhood ($p < .05$). The significance of these differences were determined using the Fisher LSD post hoc test.

Table 44

Means on Each Ranking Scale in Each Childhood Religion Group

God Representation	Role of Religion in Childhood	Mean
Loving God	Minor	6.38
	Major Positive	8.43
	Major Negative	5.78
	Major Positive & Negative	5.25
Observing God	Minor	6.62
	Major Positive	5.76
	Major Negative	6.78
	Major Negative & Positive	5.25
Absent God	Minor	4.08
	Major Positive	1.90
	Major Negative	6.22
	Major Negative & Positive	4.25
Wrathful God	Minor	2.23
	Major Positive	1.48
	Major Negative	3.33
	Major Negative & Positive	5.5

Table 45

Role of Religion Groups and the RCGT: F Ratio and Probability

Source of Variance	F-Ratio	Probability
Role of Religion in Childhood (RRC)	4.13	.0117
God Representations (GR)	30.60	.0000
Interaction (RRC and GR)	3.64	.0004

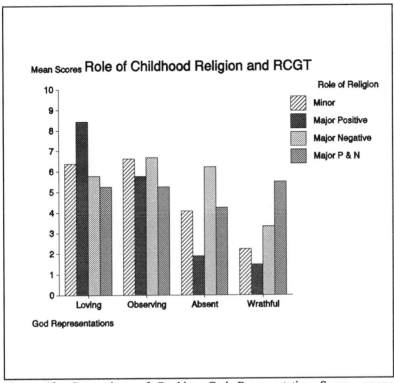

Figure 12. Comparison of Ranking God Representation Scores among Childhood Religion Groups.

As Figure 12 shows, those who described religion as playing a major positive role in their childhood had a significantly higher Ranking Loving God score than all other groups ($p < .05$). On the Ranking Observing God scale, those who described religion as playing a minor and major negative role in their childhood had significantly higher scores than those who described the role of religion in their childhood as major positive and negative ($p < .05$). On the Ranking Absent God scale, the group who described the role of religion in childhood as major positive had a significantly lower score than all other groups ($p < .05$). On the Ranking Wrathful God scale, the group who described the role of religion in childhood as major positive had a significantly lower score than those who described religion as playing a major negative ($p < .05$), and major negative and positive role in childhood ($p < .01$). The significance of these differences was determined using a Fisher LSD post hoc test.

CHAPTER FIVE

DISCUSSION

Discussion of the Major Finding

The purpose of this study was to investigate the relationship between severity of childhood traumatization and the types of God representations adults have; in particular, to investigate whether women who have histories of traumatization report more wrathful and absent God representations and less loving and observing God representations than women who have no conscious history of traumatization.

When traumatization was quantitatively measured using the Traumatic Antecedents Questionnaire, and when four types of God representations were quantitatively measured using Wootton's three God representation tasks, significant correlations were found between severity of childhood traumatization, and women's loving, absent and wrathful God representations. Further information concerning these correlations was obtained by analyses which grouped participants in terms of severity of traumatization reported. These analyses showed that women's loving, absent and wrathful God representations were consciously intact even when there was traumatization and high traumatization in childhood. When women were severely traumatized in childhood, however, loving God representations significantly decreased, while absent and wrathful God representations increased. Thus, while the initial correlational analyses demonstrated a significant relationship between severity of childhood traumatization and women's loving, absent and wrathful God representations, the repeated measures analyses of variance demonstrated that women's loving, absent and wrathful God representations were not significantly different until childhood traumatization was severe.

I would like to reflect on this major finding in terms of the three psychodynamic models of traumatization explored in the literature review. A common assumption of all three models was that traumatic stressors have a profound impact at core levels of personality, and that in traumatization powerful internal meanings and representations coalesce. These are so overwhelming that they are repressed, in as much as they can be. A review of the literature on God representations highlighted the assumption that God representations are part of the core structure of personality. How can we understand the major finding of this study, that there is a correlation between severity of childhood traumatization and women's loving, absent and wrathful God representations, but that these God representations were not significantly different until childhood traumatization was severe? I will consider this question in terms of the three psychodynamic models of traumatization and the object relations model of God representations.

Before discussing the findings in this way, it is important to note that moving from quantitative research findings to psychodynamic models involves a shift from knowledge based on experimental data to knowledge based on psychodynamic models of personality. In using the major finding of this study to reflect upon psychodynamic models of the inter-relationship between traumatization and God representations we need to be aware of the tension of moving back and forth between quantitative findings and psychodynamic models of personality.

The tension involves the degree to which one can use quantitative research findings to demonstrate aspects of psychodynamic models. The source of tension is rooted in the essential difference between experimental psychology, which works from hypotheses and the demonstration of hypotheses through quantitative research and statistical analyses, and inductive knowledge which works from psychodynamic models. The empirical truth of the major finding of this study is qualitatively different from the metaphorical truth of the models of personality (the structural model, the model of self psychology, and the object relations model). Thus, we cannot simply use the major finding to demonstrate "a piece" of the metaphorical model, as if, with enough quantitative research we could replicate one of our metaphorical models of the inter-relationship between traumatization and God representations piece by piece. Instead, we can reflect upon the consonance or dissonance between the major finding and the metaphorical models of the inter-relationship between traumatization and God representations, looking in essence at the correlation[1] between the questions and answers of the major findings, and the questions and answers of the psychodynamic models of personality.

---

[1] In using the word, correlation, I am drawing upon the revised correlational model (Tracy, 1983; Browning, 1987) in which questions and answers from our existential situation are correlated with questions and answers from Christian revelation.

The Structural Model

In a structural model of traumatization (Freud, 1926), traumatic stressors breach the so-called stimulus barrier, and the ego is flooded with intense stimulation from the external stressors. This, in turn, causes a breach in the repression barrier, and the ego is flooded with material from the unconscious---material which is normally repressed. The ego's usual functions for dealing with over-stimulation are no longer effective. The ego is not able to process what is happening, and the intrapsychic traumatization becomes like "frozen" or "undigested" material. In the immediate aftermath of traumatization, individuals experience post-traumatic stress disorder. They alternate between **re-experiencing** traumatization in intrusive flashbacks and **constricting** feelings, thoughts and memories in an effort to control such re-experiencing. In this "dialectic of opposing psychological states" (Herman, 1992, p. 47) it is as if the frozen experience of traumatization unfreezes suddenly and internally floods the psyche.

When traumatic stressors comprise a single event, then post-traumatic stress disorder may be described as simple, in that there is usually a gradual decline in intrusive symptoms although the negative symptoms of constriction and numbing may remain. If those who are traumatized are able to draw upon internal resources (available in the personality which pre-existed the traumatic event), if they are at a developmental level that gives them the most resources, and if they are part of a supportive community then they may be able to actively work on feelings, thoughts, internal representations and sensations present in flashbacks and nightmares and other experiences when traumatization intrudes. In this way the experience of traumatization is worked through, instead of dammed up and frozen.

When individuals are repeatedly exposed to traumatic stressors, then post-traumatic stress disorder becomes more complex. The more the traumatic stressors are part of a system of totalitarian control over a prolonged period of time, the more the personality changes, with alterations in affect regulation and consciousness; alterations in internal representations of one's self and the perpetrator; and alterations in systems of meaning (Herman, 1992, p. 121). These alterations profoundly affect relations with others. Included in such personality changes may be alterations in God representations (both anthropocentric and deocentric), faith systems of meaning and one's relationship with God and the community of faith. In a simple post-traumatic disorder, such alterations could be temporary, although they might be re-experienced occasionally throughout one's life, for example in nightmares or through Rorschach responses of people with post-traumatic stress disorder (van der Kolk, Blitz, Burr, Sherry, & Hartmann, 1984; van der Kolk & Ducey, 1989). The more complex the post-traumatic response, the more predominant are such alterations in God representations, faith systems of meanings, and relationships with God and the community of faith.

Using this model of the inter-relationship between traumatization and God representations, there are several ways to understand the major finding of this study, that there is a correlation between severity of childhood traumatization and women's loving, absent and wrathful God representations, but that loving, absent and wrathful God representations are not significantly different until childhood traumatization is severe. The major finding of this study can be understood as being dissonant with the structural model in that it demonstrates that traumatization and even high traumatization in childhood is not correlated with adult representations of God. Even when highly traumatized as children, the women in this sample trust and believe in a world in which God is experienced predominantly as loving. Only when there is severe childhood traumatization are these foundational beliefs absent and women envision a world in which God is experienced as absent and/or wrathful.

An explanation of the major finding of this study which is consonant with the structural model and is also supported in the literature (Johnson & Eastburg, 1992) is that all of these women except those who were severely traumatized had multivalent representations of God as loving, distant and wrathful in their childhood. Johnson and Eastburg's study did not measure degree of traumatization.[2] It could be that among their sample, the abused children were not severely traumatized, as some of the women in the present study were. One could speculate that if severity of traumatization had been measured, then Johnson and Eastburg might have found that those children who were severely traumatized had significantly different God representations than those who were less severely traumatized. In considering Johnson and Eastburg's findings alongside the findings of the present study, one might conclude that the multivalent God representations of childhood became predominantly loving in adulthood for the women in this sample, except when severe traumatization occured. When as children they were severely traumatized, multivalent God representations in childhood became predominantly absent and wrathful God representations in adulthood.

These findings may be specific to women who experience a vocation towards

---

[2]The additional finding on the correlation between role of religion in childhood and God representations while not conclusive, suggests that a major positive role of religion in childhood is significantly correlated with several of the God representation scales, such that these women have significantly higher loving God representations and significantly lower absent and wrathful God representations. One wonders whether such women would have had multivalent God concepts as children, similar to the children tested in the Johnson and Eastburg (1992) study.

theological, psychological or social work graduate studies. Among a different population, loving God representatives might not predominate when there is any history of abuse. This is the case among most of the Dutch women interviewed by Imbens and Jonker (1992). The women in the present study may represent the experience of women who have "worked through" absent and wrathful God representations, along with other psychic material associated with traumatization, such that loving God representations predominate in adulthood.

When traumatic stressors are repeated and prolonged, and part of a totalitarian system, then post-traumatic stress may become complex. In the process, there may be alterations in self perception and perceptions of God, alterations in one's relationship with God and the faith community, and alterations in faith systems. The women in this sample who were severely traumatized may have experienced these alterations as part of complex post-traumatic stress disorder. Thus, the differences in scores on the loving, absent and wrathful God representation scales may be correlated with differences on a spectrum of post-traumatic stress disorders, ranging from simple to complex:

Post-Traumatic Stress Disorder Spectrum

NO TRAUMA	TRAUMA	HIGH TRAUMA	SEVERE TRAUMA
NO PTSD	NO PTSD/SIMPLE PTSD		COMPLEX PTSD
High Loving God	High Loving God	High Loving God	Low Loving God
Low Absent God	Low Absent God	Low Absent God	High Absent God
Low Wrathful God	Low Wrathful God	Low Wrathful God	High Wrathful God

Another explanation of the major finding of this study which is consonant with the structural model is that representations of God as absent or wrathful are deeply disturbing and even those who were highly traumatized can effectively keep such representations repressed. Those who were severely traumatized cannot help but be aware of such troubling representations of an absent and wrathful God and these representations are more predominant than representations of God as loving. In other words, traumatization of any degree may provoke or enhance representations of God as absent or wrathful, but these remain for the most part repressed, along with other disturbing meanings and aspects of the traumatic event. In this sample of women, the difference between those who were severely traumatized and those who were traumatized and highly traumatized may have more to do with the repression barrier than with the degree of loving, absent and wrathful God representations. Specifically, women who were severely traumatized may experience more continuous and less sporadic breaches in the repression barrier, such that disturbing images of God as absent or wrathful are not an occasional part of their religious experience, but rather a more ongoing part of their religious experience.

A Self Psychological Model

In a self psychological model, the most profound impact of traumatization is the threat to the self and the accompanying experiences of self fragmentation which can be seen in self-state dreams that replay traumatic events. Utilizing literature on the psychology of religion, one can describe all self representations as containing implicit or explicit representations of God, that is, the internalized representations of God which have become part of the structure of the self in the course of development. For example, the sense of the self's "innate sense of vigor, greatness and perfection " (Kohut & Wolf, 1978, p. 414) may be linked with a representation of an empowering God in whose image we are created. Or a sense of safety may be linked with God as "an image of calmness, infallibility and omnipotence " (Kohut & Wolf, 1978, p. 414). What are called "the archaic narcissistic fantasies central to the organization of self-experience" (Ulman & Brothers, 1988, p. xii) contain implicit or explicit experiences of God as an all-powerful, infallible deity who protects us because we are special, beloved children of God.

When traumatic stressors and the re-experiencing of traumatic stressors threaten the self, they also threaten the very structures of the self; in particular, the images of God as loving. Specifically, God may no longer mirror and affirm but abandon and punish. God may shift from being calm to being wrathful, and omnipotence may turn malevolent. As archaic narcissistic fantasies collapse, images of God as powerful, loving and protective may also collapse. God may be experienced as powerless and absent, in the same way that the self is experienced as a vulnerable, helpless victim. Or God may be experienced as violently powerful, aligned with those who abuse.

How can we explain the finding that there is a correlation between severity of traumatization and loving, absent and wrathful God representations, but that loving, absent and wrathful God representations are not significantly different until traumatization is severe?   Several explanations are plausible. One explanation which is dissonant with the self psychological model is that traumatization does not, in fact, affect one's representation of God until it is severe. Loving God representations remain an unshakable structure until there is severe traumatization. One way to understand this is through the metaphor of an earthquake. We might suppose that one's God representations are like structures that can withstand mild and moderate earthquakes, but when an earthquake is severe enough, then these structures begin, not simply to crack, but to topple.

Another explanation of the major finding which is consonant with the self psychological model has to do more with the momentary nature of self-fragmentation. It could be that even those who were highly traumatized can, for the most part, still either maintain an ongoing sense of themselves as cohesive, or have been able to repair damage to self structures and along with that, representations of God as loving. There may be moments when the sense of self is threatened, and when God is experienced as wrathful or absent. When answering questions about God representations, however, they experience themselves for the most part as cohesive, and God as loving.[3] This may be particularly true of this sample of women, if one speculates that those who make it as far as graduate studies in theology, social work and psychology are more able to maintain a cohesive sense of self. Those who were severely traumatized are different, in that experiences of self fragmentation, and accompanying implicit experiences of God as absent or wrathful, are more ongoing and less sporadic. These women may have experienced such fragmentation when going through the God representation tasks, and this may be reflected in the descriptions of God which they chose.[4]

Just as with a structural model of traumatization, it may be that among this sample of women God representations are correlated with traumatization only when traumatization is severe. Or it may be that the differences in God representations between the severely traumatized and the other trauma groups has to do with an ongoing, rather than momentary fragmentation of self, or, as with the structural model, an ongoing, rather than momentary breaching of the repression barrier. Drawing again upon Herman's (1992) description of a post-traumatic stress disorder spectrum, we can wonder whether women experiencing simple post-traumatic stress disorder are able to repair damage to self structures and the God representations embedded in self structures. Women experiencing complex post-traumatic stress disorder may experience alterations in self structure which leave such structures prone to fragmentation, and the emergence, in fragmentation, of predominantly absent and wrathful God representations.

---

[3]It is important to note that the God representation tasks developed by Wootton, and in fact all God representation tasks reviewed in the literature, have not been tested for reliability, in that they have not been administered twice to the same sample so that scores could be compared. God representation tasks may well be sensitive to fluctuations in experiences of self cohesion.

[4]Perhaps for the severely traumatized group, some of the metaphors and adjectives describing God were evocative of their traumatic experiences, similar to how Rorschach cards were so evocative that, in responding to them, some Vietnam veterans were immersed in their traumatic experiences of combat (van der Kolk & Ducey, 1989).

An Object Relations Model

In an object relations model of traumatization, traumatization is thought to be accompanied by a coalescence of internal self and God representations linked with the traumatization. Some of these may be highly disturbing, such as representations associated with humiliating, shameful, frightening, aggressive and sexual aspects of the traumatic experience. The more disturbing the representations, the more likely they will be repressed. Fairbairn (1952) speculated that those who were sexually abused might transfer the badness of the abuser onto themselves, as a way of keeping the internalized abuser "good." They might then cope with their unconditional badness by creating a religious system in which God is in charge and their unconditional badness can be dealt with through grace, redemption, repentance and forgiveness.

In the literature review, Fairbairn's theory was elaborated using Spero's model of anthropocentric and deocentric God representations (Spero, 1992). Fairbairn is describing internal anthropocentric God representations which are formed from internalized human object representations that have coalesced during traumatization. These anthropocentric God representations are embedded in religious systems involving unconditional badness, grace, redemption and forgiveness. Such religious systems are projected onto the external environment.

Spero's model goes beyond psychologistic object relations models which describe how internal God representations are formed from internalized human object representations. Spero's model includes a real Diety object in the external environment which is internalized. Such internalization may happen directly; or through particular object representations such as parental representations; or through a myriad of internal representations. Included in Spero's model of the external environment are significant persons, such as parents, and their projected representations, as well as God and the projected representations of God.

Spero's model provides a map for understanding the research finding of this study. In the external environment are those involved in experiences of abuse: perpetrators, caretakers, siblings and others. Following Spero's model, we could add God as a being present in experiences of abuse. In the experience of traumatization and its aftermath, internal representations of those who played significant roles in the abuse are formed. If we assume that all significant internal representations are shaped by experiences of traumatization, then we must assume that God representations are shaped during traumatization, both those that are primarily anthropocentric (the internal God representations formed primarily through internalized object representations of significant relationships) and those that are primarily deocentric (the internalized God representations of a relationship with God). These internal representations of perpetrators, God, caretakers and others are projected onto the external environment. The research findings of this study highlight the loving, absent and wrathful qualities of the projected God representations and infer the presence of such qualities in internal representations associated with traumatization. Figure 13, based upon Spero's model (Spero, 1992, p. 141), depicts the inter-relationship among external figures, internal representations and projected representations.

With this figure before us, we have a model for understanding the findings of this study. This study highlights women's loving, absent and wrathful projected God representations, depicted in figure 13 by the bold circle. In seeking to understand why women's loving, absent and wrathful projected God representations are not significantly different until childhood traumatization is severe, we are making inferences about what happens to God representations during and following traumatization. Many inferences are possible. These can be put in the form of questions.

Do both anthropocentric and deocentric loving God representations remain relatively intact during and following childhood traumatization? Johnson and Eastburg's research suggests that children's projected God representations are multivalent, with no significant difference between God representations of abused and nonabused children (Johnson & Eastburg, 1992). We need to remember that they did not measure severity of abuse. If there were severely abused children in their sample, their God representations might have been significantly different. It is unclear, given the scarcity of research, whether there are significant differences in projected God representations during childhood, adolesence and adulthood of those who are not traumatized, traumatized and severely traumatized. If it were possible to measure, would these differences originate in anthropocentric and/or deocentric God representations? Are anthropocentric God representations more liable to be shaped during and after traumatization than deocentric God representations? If so, would the stability and/or later emergence of deocentric loving God representations "repair" anthropocentric God representations shaped in disturbing ways during traumatization?[5] As adults who experienced a vocation for ministry, theological studies, social work and psychology, these women may have formulated cognitive schemata of self, others and the world in which God is loving, even while they may still occasionally remember and re-experience the multivalence of their childhood God representations. It is as if they were able to salvage redemptive, beneficial aspects of their childhood experience of God and combine those with redemptive, nurturing experiences of God as adults. In this process, they may have established underlying metaphors of God as loving, which generate cognitive schemata of self, world and God in which grace and love

---

[5]Spero (1992, p. 175) in a case study suggests that as anthropocentric God representations grow and mature, the objective God is "perceived in a less endopsychically encumbered way."

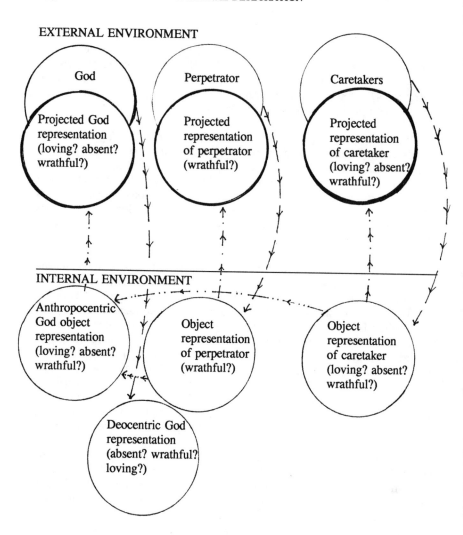

Figure 13. An Objects Relations Model of Traumatization

prevail. These women were describing their adult experience of God in doing the God representation tasks. In fact, several women, when they began the God representation tasks, asked whether they should draw upon their childhood or their adult experience of God, and commented that if they drew solely upon their childhood experience of God, their choices would be quite different.

Spero's model may also depict the role of adaptive and beneficial object representations which form during and after traumatization. Such representations may shape and enhance anthropocentric representations of God as loving. In this particular sample, it may be that many who were traumatized were able to maintain or form adaptive and beneficial representations of self and God after the traumatic event, such that these now predominate.[6] Considering that these are graduate students in theology, social work and psychology, one would suppose that this might be the case. The women who were severely traumatized may have had little which they could salvage from their childhood experiences, and less positive adult experiences with which to build new representations of God. When abuse is prolonged and repeated, internal representations may become and remain negative, such that it is no longer possible to shape anthropocentric representations of God as loving. There may even have been moments when children of prolonged and repeated abuse truly experienced God as wrathful, absent and as not loving them (shaping their deocentric God representations).[7] Or their experiences of prolonged and repeated abuse may make it seemingly impossible for them to experience the loving qualities of who God truly is.

Most of the women were able to use the metaphors, adjectives and descriptions of God as pieces of a puzzle with which they could put together their own personal images of God as loving. Those who were severely traumatized may have reacted to the loving metaphors, adjectives and descriptions of God, as being descriptions of the Judeo-Christian God that was false for them, the God who abandoned them. They may have rejected many of these images of a loving God, not because these images described God as loving, but because they were

---

[6]It is important to remember the bi-directional nature of the relationship between traumatization and God representations. Pre-existing loving God representations may lessen traumatization when they are part of an empathic experience which helps those who are abused cope with traumatic stressors. Pre-existing absent and wrathful God representations may aggravate traumatization. God representations may shape the severity of traumatization and the severity of traumatization may shape God representations.

[7]Spero (1992, p. 145) describes the dilemma of working with patients who may believe that they experience God's objective wrath. Their experience of God may contradict the therapist's experience of God as loving.

associated with an oppressive religion that was patriarchal or racist.[8]   Such speculations are supported in the scarce literature in which women who were sexually abused as children describe their predominantly negative images of God and attitudes towards their childhood religion (Poling, 1992; Imbens & Jonker, 1992).[9]

Perhaps if there had been a God representation task in which women simply created metaphors and adjectives of God rather than sorted and chose, the women who were severely traumatized would have created more images of an immanent and transcendent God who was loving.   Such a speculation highlights the limitations of "forced choice" God representation tasks, a limitation which may be particularly problematic for women who may have experienced severe traumatization and whose experience of organized religion is oppressive.   This limitation will be explored further at the conclusion of this chapter.

When one considers that there may be great inconsistencies between unconscious God representations and the projected conscious loving, absent and wrathful God representations measured in this study,[10] then the findings of this research may take on new meanings.   For example, such findings may highlight differences in the repression barriers between those who are traumatized, highly traumatized and severely traumatized, such that those who were severely traumatized were less likely to repress disturbing God representations and more likely to project such qualities onto God.

When Spero's model is combined with Fairbairn's suppositions about abuse and religious systems, then one may speculate about religious systems and projections of a loving God that arise out of abuse.   It could be that those who were traumatized did develop religious systems in which a loving God ordered a system in which unconditional badness could be ameliorated through grace, redemption and repentance.   In such a system God and the abusing parent could preserve their goodness, keeping intact a precarious trust in the world and those who order the world.   Individuals with such a system would naturally choose

---

[8]The additional findings that the God representations of the Caucasian participants were significantly different from the God representations of the Black, Hispanic and Asian participants are not conclusive, but suggest that those marginalized in our culture by their racial identity may have associated the metaphors, adjectives and characterizations with the Judeo-Christian God of oppressive hierarchies.

[9]There may be particular cultural differences in the religion of the Dutch women interviewed by Imbens and Jonker and the religions of the women interviewed in the present study.   The women in the present study represent a more heterogenous religious and cultural sample.

[10]Spero (1992, pp. 158-161) describes paradoxes in the level of religious practice, which may point to object representations that carry contradictory religious significance.   One would suppose that the more disturbing the contradictions are, the more likely they will be repressed.

loving representations of God and reject absent or wrathful representations of God.[11]   It could be that when trauma is too severe, either with too many traumatic experiences or too many abusers, such a system collapses.   In other words, such a means of coping is no longer available when traumatization exceeds a certain degree.   When that happens, then the self can no longer carry all of the badness; the system collapses, and the seemingly loving God is "unmasked" as often wrathful or absent.   The women in this study, when traumatized and even highly traumatized, can preserve or remake their experience of God as loving. With some of these women, this may indicate the depths of their faith journey. For others, this may indicate a desperate need to preserve "a good God" at a cost to themselves (as Fairbairn suggests).   When childhood violence becomes catastrophic, it is not possible for women to preserve a narrative of God as wholly loving.[12]

In elaborating Fairbairn's descriptions of the religious systems that may form during traumatization, it is helpful to remember the role of one's religious culture in shaping and reinforcing such religious systems.   An example is a culture where parents are depicted as honorable, the self as bad, God as distant and condemning, and abuse as deserved punishment.   Some psychodynamic theorists on abuse, like Alice Miller (1986), have suggested that we live in a culture in which we preserve the benevolent authority and innocence of abusing adults.   In such a cultural system, abuse goes unnamed.   This may create great pressure to preserve images of God as loving, until the violence becomes catastrophic.   To identify God with the violence may undermine the very foundations of the self, and one's basic sense of trust in the world, both at an individual level and a cultural level.   One may be left with memories of horrific suffering, chilling cruelty and inhumanity. Such memories cannot be pieced together into a narrative of a loving, benevolent God.

When we consider all three psychodynamic models of traumatization, it becomes clear that a simple interpretation of the major finding of this study which

---

[11]We may note that Wootton's scales do not allow one to distinguish between those with rigid, fundamentalist faith systems that are formed out of anxiety and shame and those with complex, flexible faith systems that allow one to cope with ambiguity.   Both of these types could have high scores on loving God scales and low scores on absent and wrathful God scales.

[12]It would be interesting to compare God representations of those who experience severe traumatization in childhood with God representations of those severely traumatized in the Holocaust.   A study comparing 125 Holocaust survivors and 189 children of survivors with 128 controls and 91 offspring found that survivors and their offspring identified themselves as religious more often than did the control group (Carmil & Breznitz, 1991).   While the authors restate this finding as Holocaust survivors and their offspring having a greater belief in God, in fact identifying oneself as religious does not necessarily indicate greater belief in God, nor how one represents God.

is dissonant with all three psychodynamic models is that traumatization in childhood is not inter-related with one's God representations in adulthood unless it is severe. A more complex conclusion which is consonant with all three models has to do with differences in simple and complex post-traumatic stress disorder, repression, self-fragmentation, the capacity to repair or reconstruct representations of God in the aftermath of traumatization, and the societal pressures on victims of abuse to maintain representations of God and parents as loving.

The additional findings describe differences in the God representations between those who said that they had an alcoholic parent and those who didn't. The experience of having an alcoholic parent has a consistent, clear relationship with a decreased experience of God as loving and an increased experience of God as absent and wrathful. These findings demonstrate the inter-relationship between an alcoholic parent and one's God representation.[13] These additional findings can best be elaborated using Spero's model of God representations (Spero, 1992, p. 141). Simply put, the findings highlight how anthropocentric God representations may be formed out of internalized representations associated with an alcoholic parent, such that parental and God representations are depicted as absent and wrathful. As with the experience of severe traumatization, the experience of having an alcoholic parent may make it difficult to repair or reconstruct representations of God as loving.

Discussion of Secondary Findings

In Wootton's study, he used the multitrait-multimethod matrices to demonstrate the convergent and discriminant validity of the loving and wrathful God scales (Wootton, 1990, p. 125). In this study, the convergent and discriminant validity of the loving, wrathful and absent God scales was demonstrated. In the heterotrait-monomethod triangles of correlations among God representation scales, there were several consistent patterns across all three methods: 1) the negative correlation between loving and absent God scales; 2) the positive correlation between the absent God and wrathful God scales. The negative correlation between loving and wrathful God representations held up for two of the three methods. These patterns demonstrated the discriminant validity of the absent, wrathful and loving God representation scales.

The convergent validity of the loving, absent and wrathful God representation scales was demonstrated with positive significant correlations between same scales

---

[13]The correlation between having an alcoholic parent and God representations was not part of the hypotheses of this research design. They are included more as suggestive findings and as an avenue for further research.

across the three methods. In the third measure of validity, when the correlation of a particular scale across methods was compared with the correlations of the same scale with other scales in the same method, the Wootton Metaphor Characterization of God Task came out with the strongest patterns of validity, although the high correlation between loving and wrathful God representations weakened this demonstration of validity. Finally, a pattern of scale inter-relationships with the loving, absent and wrathful God representation scales was demonstrated across all methods.

In conclusion, one can state that this research project demonstrates the convergent and discriminant validity of the loving, absent and wrathful God scales. One may also utilize correlational patterns in other analyses of the study to demonstrate the validity of these scales. When an analysis of variance was utilized to study the mean God representation scores of trauma groups, the similar patterns in mean scores across methods strikingly demonstrated how each scale (loving, absent and wrathful) was consistent across methods. The same can be said for the analysis of variance utilized to study alcoholic and non alcoholic parent groups, ethnic groups, and role of childhood religion groups.

This leaves one with the question of why Wootton's original study failed to demonstrate the validity of the absent God scale when this scale proved to be the most valid scale in this study. It may be that the age and life experience of his sample was such that they had not experienced God as absent, and thus did not draw upon any of these experiences when doing God representation tasks. The women in my sample may have had more life experiences of God as absent, particularly in their experiences of trauma. A major finding of this study is that the absent God scales, as Wootton has constructed them, are valid and need to be included in further research utilizing Wootton's three God representation tasks.

The findings of this study corroborated Wootton's findings that the observing God scale cannot be demonstrated as valid, either with a multitrait-multimethod analysis, or through other analyses, like the repeated measures analysis of variance. Wootton created this scale as a way of describing "the God who is good but not as active and strong as the Loving God" (Wootton, 1990, p. 71). It may be that what was needed was not a God who was more distant and less active and strong, but a transcendent God (in contrast with all the metaphors of an immanent God that made up the loving God scales) who was equally active and strong, but in a transcendent rather than immanent relationship. There is ample religious literature on transcendent images of God. Indeed, one could describe the most predominant images of God in the Hebrew Bible as one of a mysterious, transcendent, creative presence. It may well be that Wootton's metaphors, adjectives and descriptions of God as loving adequately capture the sense of an immanent God, who can be likened to and experienced as incarnate in our most nurturing, intimate, soothing relationships.   His metaphors, adjectives and descriptions of an observing God, drawing upon human analogies as they do (for example, "the director sitting in the audience on opening night," "a biologist looking into a microscope," "an astronomer gazing into a telescope") may not capture the experience of a transcendent God who is our ground of being, whose over-arching presence is in all and through all, and whose majesty and creativity is mediated through beauty, nature and the arts.   Indeed, when one reviews the observing God metaphors and adjectives, one is struck by the paucity of language to describe this quality of God.   This may be one reason why this scale did not prove to be valid.

The observing God metaphors highlight another limitation with the observing God scale.   Out of the 15 metaphors, 4 are images of machines and an animal (a clock, a camera, an owl, and a satellite), 7 are associated traditionally with men (an astronomer, a photographer, a biologist, an accountant, a theatrical director, a night watchman, a team owner) and 4 are ambiguous in terms of gender (an artist, a librarian, a figure, a census taker).   The predominance of male metaphors may create the ambiguity which Wootton (1990, p. 180) noted, that the observing God metaphors may allude to a more malevolent rather than benevolent quality of observing.

Wootton speculated that the <u>Wootton Metaphor Characterization of God Task</u> may be "most attuned to the level of "unconscious processes" in the assessment of the God representation" (Wootton, 1990, p. 194).   He noted that "the discursive methods employed by the <u>Adjective Characterization of God Task</u> and the <u>Wootton Adjusted Ranking Characterization of God Task</u>" may draw upon conscious images of God, while "highly figurative language, as found in metaphors, possesses a more symbolic function" and may draw upon more unconscious levels of God representations (Wootton, 1990, p. 190).   Wootton supports this claim in two ways.   First, social desirability was less of a factor for the <u>WMCGT</u> than the other scales.   Second, there were different patterns of inter-relationships among dependent and independent variables with this method than the other two methods.   The results of this research project does not support this particular finding.   There was no difference in the degree to which social desirability affected scores on the <u>Wootton Metaphor Characterization of God Task</u> as compared with the other two methods.   As well, in all the various repeated measures analyses of variance undertaken, there was no difference in patterns of inter-relationships among dependent and independent variables with the metaphor God representation task as compared with the other two God representation tasks.

Limitations of This Study

The major limitations of this study concern sample homogeneity, instruments and methodology. This exploratory study did not control for factors such as vocation and history of treatment. The complexities of these factors become most evident when one considers the homogeneity of this sample and limitations in generalizability. This sample consisted of female graduate students studying social work, psychology and theology. The major findings of this study may well be unique to this particular group. For example, we cannot conclude that male graduate students would show a similar pattern in God representations scores, since there is a complex interaction between gender identity and experiences of violence in our culture.

Besides gender, another characteristic of this sample which limits generalizability is their common vocation of being in graduate degree programs in helping professions. The findings of this study and its clinical implications of may only be relevant when one is working with female social workers, psychologists or ministers. More importantly, aspects of this vocational calling may play a crucial role in shaping one's images of God (and images of God may play a crucial role in shaping one's vocation). Among a less heterogenous sample, one might find that women experiencing any level of traumatization in childhood have God representations that are as less loving and more absent and wrathful (as the women in Imbens and Jonker's (1992) study did).

Another limitation of the study concerns instrumentation. The Traumatic Antecedents Questionnaire is limited in that it is a simple way of quantitatively measuring the complex phenomenon of traumatization. It does attempt to approximate the compounding effects of prior traumatization and developmental phase. However, it does not measure the degree to which traumatization is compounded by factors such as empathic neglect (what van der Kolk (1987) identifies as the role of the social support system), pre-existing personality, genetic predisposition and severity of traumatic stressors. Another limitation of this instrument is that it defines violence as sexual abuse, physical abuse, and witnessing domestic violence. The instrument does not recognize experiences of emotional abuse or neglect. What this means in terms of the study's findings is that the Traumatic Antecedents Questionnaire under-estimates severity of traumatization when there is no social support, when traumatic stressors are severe, when pre-existing personality and genetic predisposition compound traumatization, and when there is emotional abuse and neglect. The Traumatic Antecedents Questionnaire may over-estimate severity of traumatization when there is a social support system that provides support and helps create meaning immediately after the traumatic stressors occur, or when pre-existing personality (which may include empowering loving God representations) and genetic predisposition give one resources to cope with traumatic stressors so that they are not so overwhelming.

There are several limitations with the instruments developed for measuring God representations. A major limitation is that these instruments are designed to measure conscious God representations. As a survey of the literature has shown, disturbing God representations, disturbing qualities of traumatization and disturbing inter-relationships between trauma and God representations are likely to be repressed. Another limitation is that none of the God representation measures have been tested for reliability. It may be that the God representations one chooses may be strongly influenced by the state one is in. On one occasion one might have high loving, low absent and wrathful God representation scores. On another occasion one might have low loving, high absent and wrathful God representation scores.

A second limitation with instrumentation concerns the difficulties with demonstrating the validity of the observing God scales. When such difficulties are considered, it becomes apparent that what may be needed is a scale that adequately describes a sense of God's transcendence.

Another limitation with the God representation scales is that they utilize a forced-choice format. Such a format may be associated with oppressive experiences of a patriarchal church. An open-ended format in which women choose their own metaphors and adjectives of God may draw upon a more open and creative spirituality, especially among women and women of color. Such a format may result in quite different God representations than in a forced-choice format.

Finally, a limitation of this study is in its quantitative methodology. The major findings highlight the complexities of the inter-relationship between God representations and traumatization, but the methodology does not allow one to explore the contents of this inter-relationship. As well, the discussion of the major finding highlights the tensions of moving from empirical knowledge to inductive knowledge that utilizes metaphorical models. While the discussion of the major finding demonstrates a way of moving from one kind of knowledge to the other, it also highlights the need for 1) research approaches that use "whatever approaches are responsive to the particular questions and subject matter addressed" (Polkinghorne, 1983, p. 3) and 2) using multiple procedures for research designs.[14]

---

[14]Polkinghorne (1983, p. 252) gives a good example of this:
   A single topic---anxiety, for example---might be approached with the hermeneutic, the systemic, the phenomenological, and the statistically linked measurement systems of

Areas for Further Research

The major finding of this study, that there is a correlation between severity of childhood traumatization and women's loving, absent and wrathful God representations, but that loving, absent and wrathful God representations are not significantly different until traumatization is severe, suggests many avenues of further research. Obviously, the first avenue of further research is to replicate these findings with other sample groups that include men and people from a variety of educational, vocational, ethnic and faith backgrounds. An important aspect of replication is to plan on dividing the sample into trauma groups from the outset and to see whether the same correlational patterns hold true when other factors such as gender, educational level, vocation and ethnicity vary. As was reported in the additional findings of this study, there were some significant God representation differences between ethnic groups. While the size of the sample was not large enough for this finding to be conclusive, it does highlight a need to utilize the God representation tasks again with a diverse ethnic groups.

A second avenue of further research is to use this quantitative study of traumatization and God representations as a first step in developing a multi-method research design that uses a variety of research methodologies to study the inter-relationship of traumatization and God representations. This type of "syncretic research" is more than a matter of collating research results from different methodologies. It involves "the additional step of syncretizing the results of the multiple inquiries into a unified and integral result" (Polkinghorne, 1983, p. 254). As part of this syncretic approach to the study of traumatization and God representations, a qualitative methodology can be used to explore the common themes that emerge when one asks women and men to reflect on the inter-relationship between childhood experiences of traumatization and God representations. A qualitative methodology would allow one to explore the highly idiosyncratic nature of both traumatization and God representations, and might encourage women and men to explore dimensions of their spirituality that may not be accessed when using a forced-choice format to describe God representations.

Another avenue of further research which is part of a syncretic approach to investigating the relationship between traumatization and God representations is to develop methodologies for exploring the unconscious dimensions of both traumatization and God representations. This can be done through projective techniques and working with dreams. For example, the Early Memories Test (Mayman, 1968) might be adapted to explore one's earliest memories associated with God or might be used to infer what one's earliest experiences of God were.

---

inquiry... Each of these systems of inquiry is able to detect and describe some aspects of anxiety, but each of them also misses parts of the full experience.

Since two of the assumptions of this test are that early memories reveal images of the self in relation to others, and that early memories reveal underlying themes about peoples' representational worlds, this test could be used to infer images of the self in relation to God, and underlying themes about God. Similarly, the Object Representation Scale for Dreams (Krohn & Mayman, 1974) could also be used to infer deep, underlying metaphors of self, God and others. A systematic, thematic analysis of the texts of dreams and early memories could be used in a qualitative research design to highlight the underlying metaphors of God and self that become entwined when there is traumatization. There is great potential for using Rorschach cards as a projective technique for exploring object representations, as Urist (1977) does, and also for exploring the ongoing disturbances caused by traumatization, as van der Kolk and Ducey (1989) do.

Another aspect to future research on traumatization and God representations that uses a syncretic approach involves a theoretical model in which object relations theory is interfaced with cognitive developmental theory. The combined use of object relations measures with measures of cognitive schemata could highlight the way traumatization affects God, self and other representations at various levels: the deep structural level of object relations, and the complex cognitive schemata of self, others and God. For example, projective measures for exploring underlying object representations could be used in conjunction with Janoff-Bulman's World Assumptions Scale (Janoff-Bulman, 1989a) to explore the consonance or dissonance between representations of self, God and others and complex cognitive schemata of self, God and others. Such research, when undertaken with those who have been traumatized, may help us to understand more fully the unconscious dimensions of traumatization and how these may be consonant or dissonant with complex schemata of self, God and others.

A final area of further research is to continue utilizing the God representation tasks developed by Wootton. When these scales were first used with a sample of 101 undergraduate students (Wootton, 1990) the validity of the absent God scales could not be demonstrated. In the present study, with female graduate students ranging in age from 21 to 58 years old, the absent God scales proved to be the most valid of all four scales. Clearly, further research utilizing these God representation tasks can further demonstrate the validity of these instruments. In addition, there is a need for exploring whether a scale measuring the transcendent dimensions of God could be developed.

CHAPTER SIX

CONCLUSIONS

Research Significance of This Study

The initial correlational analyses between severity of traumatization and God representations showed significant relationships between severity of childhood traumatization and women's loving, absent and wrathful God representations, in the directions predicted. When these correlations were explored further using a repeated measures analysis of variance, it was demonstrated that women's loving, absent and wrathful God representations were not significantly different until childhood traumatization was severe. How do these findings confirm or contradict research on traumatization and God representations?

The inter-relationship between severe traumatization and God representations has been demonstrated in the limited research on multiple personality disorders (Higdon & Faheem, 1984; Bowman, Coons, Jones & Oldstrom, 1987; Bowman, 1989). The major finding of the present study confirms the inter-relationship between experiences of severe abuse and God representations.

There is ample research literature on the relationship between God and parental object relationships (Stephenson, 1953; Strunk, 1959; Godin & Hallez, 1964; Spilka et al., 1964; Gorsuch, 1968; Nelson, 1971; Tamayo & Desjardins, 1976; Tamayo & Duga, 1977; Vergote & Tamayo, 1981; Pasquali, 1981; Heinrichs, 1982; Justice, 1984; Justice & Lambert, 1986; Johnson & Eastburg, 1992). Among these studies, Justice (1984) and Justice and Lambert (1986) considered the role of abusive parents and found a correlation between abusive parents and negative God representations. Johnson and Eastburg (1992) found that both the abused and nonabused children of their sample group described multivalent God representations that were kind, distant and wrathful. The abused children's parental representations were less kind and more wrathful than the nonabused children's representations. They concluded that parental, but not God concepts, are significantly correlated with abuse during childhood. They suggest that a correlation between abusive parents and God representations may only appear later in development, or that God and parental representations may develop independently.

The major finding of the present study highlights the inter-relationship between severe childhood violence, all of which involved abusive parents, and women's loving, absent and wrathful God representations. This finding may be related to two aspects of the research design of this study: measuring severity of traumatization, and the sample's common vocation of graduate studies in theology, social work and theology. Severity of traumatization may be a significant factor for this particular sample, or may have been a significant factor for the sample groups of Justice and Lambert (1986) and Johnson and Eastburg (1992) had they measured severity of abuse. A conclusion that draws together these research findings is that the multivalent God representations of childhood may develop into primarily loving God representations among those who are not abused and those who are abused but not severely abused. The primarily absent and wrathful God representations arise among those who are severely abused.

The unique contribution of this study to the research on the inter-relationship between God and parental object relations lies in the finding that among the women of this sample loving, absent and wrathful God representations are not significantly different until childhood traumatization is severe. In discussing this finding, Spero's model (Spero, 1992, p. 141) was used to understand the internalization of those in the external environment during experiences of abuse---perpetrators, caretakers, and God. What was measured in the present study was the loving, wrathful and absent qualities of women's conscious projected God representations. When these projected God representations were used to infer the inter-relationship between internal representations of God and parents, then what was glimpsed was the way severe traumatization causes parental representations and anthropocentric God representations to share qualities of wrath and absence. The findings of this study may well illustrate the inter-relationship between internalized parental objects shaped by severe traumatization and anthropocentric God representations. A further inference from the finding of this study was that traumatization and even high traumatization does not cause parental and anthropocentric God representations to share qualities of wrath and absence; rather God remains (or is reconstructed as) primarily loving, at least at a conscious level. It must be noted that this finding may be particular to women with vocations in helping professions such as psychology, social work, and ministry.

Spero's model provides an elaboration and expansion of theoretical literature and case study analyses which describe how God representations are formed as people move through developmental phases (McDargh, 1983; Rizzuto, 1974, 1976, 1979, 1982; Meissner, 1984; Randour & Bondanza, 1987). This quantitative study demonstrates how the life event of repeated, prolonged abuse resulting in severe traumatization is inter-related with one's projected God representations, specifically, loving, absent and wrathful representations. While one cannot generalize from the experience of repeated prolonged abuse to other life events, this research finding and model do suggest that various types of life events can be studied in terms of their inter-relationship with projected God representations.

The finding of this study is consonant with recent literature on traumatization that posits a spectrum of post-traumatic stress disorders. The finding that women's projected loving, absent and wrathful God representations do not differ until childhood traumatization is severe may well illustrate the differences between simple and complex post-traumatic stress disorder. The diagnostic criteria Herman (1992, p. 121) proposes for complex post-traumatic stress disorder may be interfaced with Spero's object relations model. Figure 14 depicts the ways in which prolonged, repeated abuse in a totalitarian relationship may (1) distort internal representations of self, perpetrator, others and the anthropocentric God representations formed out of these; (2) create projections that interfere in relations with others and with God; (3) create systems of meaning that destroy faith, confirm hopelessness and despair, and enhance negative God representations, making it very difficult to have a relationship with a divine being.

The findings of this study raise questions concerning recent models of traumatization which interface object relations theory with cognitive development (Janoff-Bulman, 1985, 1989a, 1989b, 1992; McCann & Pearlman, 1990). In the sample studied, severity of childhood traumatization was correlated with loving, absent and wrathful projected representations of God. Janoff-Bulman's findings that victims differed significantly from non victims in terms of cognitive schemata of self, world and others (Janoff-Bulman, 1989a) are seemingly at odds with the finding that victims' projected God representations did not differ significantly from non victims' God representations until traumatization was severe; that is, until abuse was repeated and prolonged throughout childhood. The difference between her findings and the findings of this study may originate in differences in research design. The initial finding of this study indicated a correlation between severity of traumatization and loving, absent and wrathful God representations---a parallel finding to Janoff-Bulman's. It was only after the sample group was categorized according to severity of traumatization that it became clear that there were no significant differences among God representations of the no trauma, trauma and high trauma groups. Measuring severity of traumatization and also this sample's common vocation of graduate studies in psychology, social work and theology may make the findings of this study different from Janoff-Bulman's study.

EXTERNAL ENVIRONMENT
(Past external environment includes a history of prolonged and repeated abuse within a relationship in which the perpetrator exercised totalitarian control)

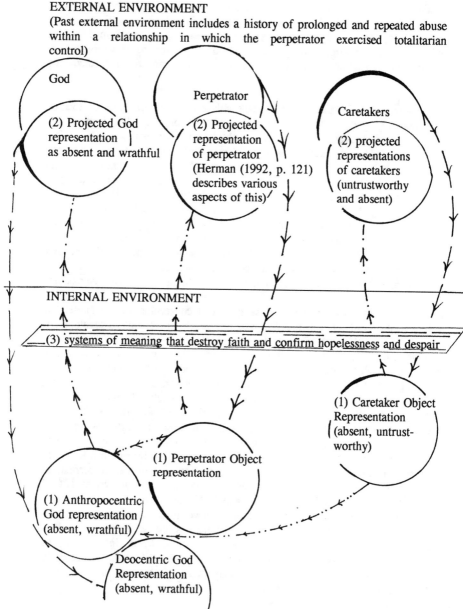

Figure 14. The Effects of Prolonged Abuse on Internal Object Representations.

One way to understand the inter-relationship between traumatization, cognitive schemata and God representations is through a model of personality wherein object representations of self, God and others lie at the deepest level of personality and give rise to cognitive schemata of self, world and others[1]. Cognitive schemata described by Janoff-Bulman correspond with the systems of meaning described by Herman (1992, p. 121), and depicted in figure 14 as a filter which shapes both what one takes in from external objects and what one projects onto external objects. Janoff-Bulman's finding, that violence altered cognitive schemata of self, world and others, is dissonant with the finding of this study, that traumatization did not alter loving, absent and wrathful projected God representations until it was severe. This dissonance causes us to question the inter-relationships among cognitive schemata of self, world and others (#3 in figure 14), internal representations (#1 in figure 14) and projected representations (#2 in figure 14). How much consonance or dissonance is there among cognitive schemata, internal representations and projected representations? Is dissonance more likely to be masked by repression?

Discussion of the research significance of the major finding of this study highlights the complexity of doing research on intrapsychic phenomenon such as traumatization, God representations and projected God representations. Spero's model helps us appreciate the complexities of infering conscious and unconscious God representations from projected God representations, such as are measured in this study. Further research on the inter-relationship of traumatization and God representations will be enhanced by the interfacing of models, for example, Herman's (1992, p. 121) model of complex post-traumatic stress disorder and Spero's (1992, p. 141) model of external objects, anthropocentric and deocentric God representations.

Clinical Significance of This Study

Research on the relationship between traumatization and God representations can enhance and enrich the work of pastoral clinicians with those who have been traumatized. While the major finding of this study demonstrates the inter-relationship between severe traumatization and projected God representations, a discussion of this finding highlights the complex interactions between severity of traumatization, internal representations of those associated with the traumatization, anthropocentric God representations, deocentric God representations, projected God representations, and the role of repression. In discussing the clinical significance of the findings, it will be helpful to interface clinical literature on

---

[1]Spero (1992, p. 139) provides helpful models for understanding the role of schema in shaping object representations.

post-traumatic stress disorder and God representations, notably, the writings of Herman (1992) and Spero (1992).[2]

Herman (1992) describes three stages of recovery from traumatization: establishment of safety, remembrance and mourning, and reconnection with ordinary life. In terms of the women who participated in this study, those who consciously represented God as predominantly loving may draw upon such representations in creating safety, remembering and mourning childhood experiences of abuse and in reconnecting with ordinary life. Those who represented God as predominantly absent and/or wrathful may have great difficulty forming safe, intimate relationships. Without a context for safety, women who represented God as predominantly absent and/or wrathful may find the task of remembering their abuse overwhelmingly painful and frightening. The differences in recovery between those with predominantly loving God representations and those with predominantly absent and/or wrathful God representations can be explored more fully by considering each stage of recovery.

In the first stage, when establishing safety is crucial, clients may be able to draw upon representations of a loving God, who created their bodies as good and who made human relationships and sexuality to be life-giving. Drawing upon God representations to help establish safety is complex, however, because unconscious dimensions of the client's God representations may be malevolent. As was highlighted when exploring the writings of Fairbairn (1952), it is difficult to determine when these loving God representations are part of a repressive intrapsychic and cultural system, in which "badness" is transferred from the abuser or from God onto the self, or when loving God representations are part of a meaning system in which the complexities of the inter-relationship between God and childhood violence are fully faced, rather than repressed. Careful attention to dreams and associations may help to highlight the disturbing dimensions of God representations.

For example, a client associated images of God as father with her physically abusive father, who could hit her at any moment. In trying to create order out of the chaos of violence, she constructed a complex rule system that would make violence predictable and help her avoid "punishment." In her adult life, she worked hard at creating the same rule system in her religion. She described overwhelming events as God "whacking her across the head." She did, however, have positive representations of Jesus and used his name as a mantra that helped

---

[2]A more complex discussion of the clinical significance of the findings would include a discussion of transference manifestations among those who are traumatized and how God representations may be embedded in such transferences. For a discussion of transference manifestations among those who are sexually abused, see Rothstein (1986).

her relax and feel safe at night. It was important, in the first stage of establishing safety, to realize that representations associated with God as father were not ultimately safe, while those associated with Jesus were.

As safety is established, clients can move into the next phase of recovery: reconstructing their memories of abuse. Pastoral counselors can encourage those who have been traumatized to fully explore the ways in which God representations and the meanings of traumatic events were formed in the aftermath of traumatization. This will be part of remembering and mourning aspects of abuse that shaped their representations of God and their meaning systems. Meaning systems may have "sprung up" as means of coping, like hastily built shelters that are thrown together after an earthquake. Together, counselor and client can consider whether these hastily constructed meaning systems became fixed and rigid or whether adult experiences were used to slowly build new structures of complex meaning. They can also explore how the presence or absence of an attuned, empathic community was the context in which meaning systems were built.

Pastoral clinicians who work with those who are traumatized can utilize the model proposed in this study, which interfaces object relations theory, particularly Spero's model of both anthropocentric and deocentric God representations, with Herman's (1992) model of a trauma spectrum ranging from simple to complex post-traumatic stress disorder. They can be sensitive to how traumatization may bring together anthropocentric God representations which are loving, absent and/or wrathful. If such God representations were part of a traumatic experience that did not fit into existing conceptual schemata, they may be "organized on a sensorimotor or iconic level---as horrific images, visceral sensations, or as fight/flight/freeze reactions" (van der Kolk, 1987, p. 282). When encoded in sensorimotor form, God representations will find expression, not in words or cognitive schemata, but in anxiety attacks and panic disorders. Anthropocentric God representations embedded at sensorimotor or iconic levels may be dissociated from and/or dissonant with other internal representations of God and may interfere with one's relationship with God, the formation of deocentric God representations and the formation of anthropocentric God representations that enhance health.

With this model, clinicians can be sensitive to the power of deep underlying representations associated with childhood and adolescent traumatization, and how these representations may shape religious or existential schemata of the self, God and others which are rigid. As Fish-Murray, Koby and van der Kolk (1987, p. 101) noted in their comparison of severely abused and non abused children, their strongest finding was that the abused children showed inflexibility of organized schemata and structures in all cognitive domains. As adults they may have fixed religious systems as their only means of coping with the representations associated with traumatization, which lie at the deepest level of their personalities.

The finding on significantly higher absent God representation scores for the severely traumatized may have clinical significance, particularly in the stages of establishing safety, and also remembering and mourning what happened. Representations of God as absent may be linked with the experience of empathic neglect that may have followed traumatic stressors (Doehring, 1993). Such experiences of absence and neglect may make it difficult to establish a sense of safety, not simply in pastoral counseling relationships and communities of faith, but indeed in the world. As well, the degree to which women can allow painful aspects of their traumatization to become known may be shaped by a shift from experiencing God as absent to experiencing God as present and loving. Analysts working with adults who were sexually abused as children report the general clinical experience that sexual abuse is often contained within the larger experience which they describe, problematically, I believe, as maternal deprivation. In working with such clients, these clinicians found that the deprivation was addressed first, before the memories of abuse surfaced (Burland & Raskin, 1990).[3] Pastoral counselors can be sensitive to the need for creating an empathic relationship in which issues of absence and neglect can be addressed, perhaps specifically the felt absence of God in the experience of traumatization.

When anthropocentric representations of an absent God are addressed in pastoral counseling, this may clear the way for anthropocentric representations of a wrathful God. As this study has demonstrated, women who were severely traumatized had significantly higher scores on wrathful God scales. The condemning, punitive, angry God may be associated with self representations of guilt, shame and fear and representations of the perpetrator as wrathful. Such representations may be too painful to face until an empathic relationship has been established, and God has been experienced as present, attuned and caring. Simply put, representations of an absent God may emerge during the first stages of recovery when issues of safety are predominant. Representations of a wrathful God may emerge when experiences of abuse are remembered. A dynamic of mourning may involve acknowledging the impact of such anthropocentric wrathful God representations on a woman's life.

One aspect of recovery from trauma may be the emergence of anthropocentric absent and wrathful God representations. Such representations may "masquerade" as God and may be part of psychic forces and representations associated with traumatization that act as gods within the inner sanctum of the personality. Recovery will involve confronting these false gods, unmasking them,

---

[3]Bernstein (1990) describes this as introjecting the supportive, maternal object.

and divesting them of their internal power.[4] Spero (1992, p. 146) describes this process as a folding back of displaced and distorted images of God, allowing one a glimpse of the objective God. Commenting on the task of forming cognitive systems of meaning complex enough to hold the full experience of violence, Herman (1992, p. 178) says that

> The traumatic event challenges an ordinary person to become a theologian... She stands mute before the emptiness of evil, feeling the insufficiency of any known system of explanation.

All in all, the discussion of the major finding of this study points to the complexities of working with the meaning systems of those who have been traumatized, and highlights how experiences of God as loving, absent and wrathful may powerfully shape the stages of recovery. The metaphor of traumatization as a desecration of the inner sanctum and the smashing of internal representations of God is a potent way to describe the impact of traumatization on one's God representations and systems of religious meaning. Recovery involves first creating safety and trust, enough to empower one to return to the scene of desecration. Next, one must sift through the rubble and reconstruct the experience of desecration, while mourning the loss of the inner sanctum and all that was associated with it. The final stage of recovery will be to build new inner sanctums and reconsecrate them. Reconsecration may happen in the ordinary moments of reconnecting with everyday life, when one experiences the sanctity of life, the blessedness of creation, and the goodness of one's body. Sexton (1975) describes such moments:

> There is joy
> in all:
> in the hair I brush each morning,
> in the Cannon towel, newly washed,
> that I rub my body with each morning,
> in the chapel of eggs I cook
> each morning...
> All this is God.

---

[4]Jordan (1986) uses the metaphor of pastoral counseling as taking on the gods, those psychic forces that masquerade as God in the aftermath of trauma.

Significance in Terms of the Community of Faith

It is important, in working with issues of violence, to move beyond the intrapsychic and interpersonal dimensions of care and healing, and address cultural dimensions of care and healing. The cultural dimensions can be addressed by considering the significance of these findings for the community of faith.

When the complexities of the inter-relationship between traumatization and violence were explored, I conjectured on the role of the community in providing a social context which may either encourage or discourage awareness of the inter-relationship between representations of God and childhood violence. Literature on the church's role in experiences of childhood abuse has demonstrated that historically the church has condoned cultural attitudes in which abuse was named as discipline and punishment. Judeo-Christian culture has often depicted parents as wholly honourable and loving, abuse as punishment for being "bad", and God as aligned with parental authority. Such religious cultures create meaning systems that are internalized by those experiencing abuse (Spero, 1992, p. 138). Even today, in some religious communities such religious systems have been elaborated to justify horrendous physical abuse of children, as Greven (1990) chillingly describes. Many religious systems maintained the cultural taboo on speaking about sexual abuse (Fortune, 1983; Brown & Bohn, 1989). The church's silence on childhood abuse has meant that traumatization was compounded by the church's neglect of those who were abused. When the church is silent, then it is more likely to be associated with the experience of an absent, condemning, distant and wrathful God. When the community of faith is silent, it stands with the perpetrator, and may join with the perpetrator in naming reality (Herman, 1992, p. 8). When the faith community is silent, "the active process of bearing witness inevitably gives way to the active process of forgetting" (Herman, 1992, p. 9).

When the community of faith stands with those who are abused, then healing and justice become possible:

> The solidarity of a group provides the strongest protection against terror and despair, and the strongest antidote to traumatic experience. Trauma isolates; the group recreates a sense of belonging. Trauma shames and stigmatizes; the group bears witness and affirms. (Herman, 1992, p. 214)

Using the metaphor of desecration, one can understand how a community of faith may provide the experience of sanctuary, religious rituals, symbols, and God representations which are internalized in the process of reconstructing the inner sanctum and reconsecrating it. Indeed, when the community of faith is immediately present in the aftermath of violence, as Herman (1992, p. 214) describes, then they "loan" a sense of sanctuary to victims, in the way that caretakers loan their psychological structures to an overwhelmed child and so contain a temporary sense of desecration and violation.

The community of faith can be challenged to seek repentance for the suffering caused by its maintenance and elaboration of religious systems that justified abuse, and its neglect of those who experienced childhood abuse. Part of this task of repentance involves facing the inter-relationship between childhood abuse and experiences of God, and developing complex meaning systems that can begin to make sense of this inter-relationship. For example, biblical studies on sexual violence and images of God as absent and wrathful can be utilized to address the inter-relationship between God and childhood experiences of abuse. Biblical studies by Trible (1984) and Bal (1988) are examples of such resources. As well, the implications of many aspects of traditional theological systems, such as suffering, divine power, divine child abuse (that is, the meaning of God sacrificing his son, and asking Abraham to sacrifice his son), patriarchy and sexuality need to be considered in the meaning systems we offer those who were abused as children. Theologians are beginning to explore such issues as they relate to experiences of sexual abuse, physical abuse and domestic violence (Brown & Bohn, 1989; Poling, 1992; Graham, 1992). Finally, we need to utilize the rich worship resources that have been created as women and men have begun to voice the prayers that arise out of experiences of violence (an example of these can be found in Fortune, 1987).

When such meaning systems are available to victims of abuse, they will not simply stand "mute before the emptiness of evil, feeling the insufficiency of any known system of explanation" (Herman, 1992, p. 178). Biblical studies, theological systems of meaning and rich worship resources may help to create the faith systems that make possible intimate, life-giving relationships with God and others.

The community of faith plays a crucial role in experiences of childhood violence. Historically, it has been a role of silence, neglect, and elaborating systems of abuse. The challenge it faces is to become a community in which violence is named, victims and abusers are cared for, and the community as a whole struggles to make sense of where God is in childhood abuse. The ultimate purpose of research on God representations and childhood traumatization is to deepen our capacity for empathy as a community of faith and to seek healing of the wounds of violence, not only as they have been experienced by individuals, but by the whole of God's creation.

BIBLIOGRAPHY

American Psychiatric Association. (1987). Diagnostic and statistical manual of mental disorders (3rd ed., rev.). Washington, DC: Author.

Armatas, P. J. (1962). A factor-analytic study of patterns of religious belief in relation to prejudice. Unpublished doctoral dissertation. University of Denver, Denver.

Bal, M. (1988). Death and dissymmetry: The politics of coherence in the Book of Judges. Chicago, IL: The University of Chicago Press.

Bell, M. D. (1988). An introduction to the Bell object relations reality testing inventory. West Haven, CT: Author.

Benson, P. & Spilka, B. (1973). God image as a function of self-esteem and locus of control. Journal for the Scientific Study of Religion, 12, 297-310.

Beres, D. & Joseph, E. (1970). The concept of mental representation in psychoanalysis. International Journal of Psychoanalysis. 51, 1-9.

Bernstein, A. (1990). The impact of incest trauma on ego development. In H. B. Levine (Ed.), Adult analysis and childhood sexual abuse (pp. 65-91). Hillsdale, NJ: The Analytic Press.

Billington, R. J. & Bell, M. D. (1985). Manual for the Bell Object Relations and Reality Testing Inventory (BORRTI) (2nd ed.). West Haven, CT: Authors.

Blatt, S. J. (1974). Levels of object relations in anaclitic and introjective depressions. Psychoanalytic Study of the Child, 29, 109-157.

Blatt, S. J. (1975). The validity of projective techniques and their research and clinical contribution. Journal of Personality Assessment, 39, 327-343.

Blatt, S. J., Brenneis, C. B., Schimek, J.G. & Glick, M. (1976). Normal development and psychological impairment of the concept of the object on the Rorschach. Journal of Abnormal Psychology, 85, 364-373.

Blatt, S. & Lerner, H. D. (1983). The psychological assessment of object representation. Journal of Personality Assessment, 47, 7-28.

Blum, H. P. (1987). The role of identification in the resolution of trauma: The Anna Freud Memorial Lecture. Psychoanalytic Quarterly, 56, 609-627.

Bowman, E. S. (1989). Understanding and responding to religious material in the therapy of multiple personality disorder. Dissociation, 2, 231-238.

Bowman, E. S., Coons, P. M., Jones, R. S. & Oldstrom, M. (1987). Religious psychodynamics in multiple personalities: Suggestions for treatment. American Journal of Psychotherapy, 41, 542-554.

Bradford, D. T. (1990). Early Christian martyrdom and the psychology of depression, suicide and bodily mutilation. Psychotherapy, 27, 30-41.

Brende, J. O. (1983). A psychodynamic view of character pathology in Vietnam combat veterans. Bulletin of the Menninger Clinic, 47, 193-216.

Brende, J. O. & Parson, E. R. (1985). Vietnam veterans: The road to recovery. New York: Plenum Press.

Brill, N. Q. (1967). Gross stress reactions: Traumatic war neuroses. In A. M. Freedman & H. L. Kaplan (Eds.), Comprehensive textbook of psychiatry. Baltimore, MD: Williams & Wilkins Co.

Brown, J. C. & Bohn, C. R. (1989). Christianity, patriarchy and abuse. New York: Pilgrim Press.

Browning, D. (1987). Mapping the terrain of pastoral theology: Toward a practical theology of care. Pastoral Psychology, 36, 10-27.

Browning, D. (1988). Religious ethics and pastoral care. Philadelphia, PA: Fortress Press.

Browning, D. (1991). A fundamental practical theology. Minneapolis, MN: Fortress Press.

Burgess, A. W. & Holmstrom, L. L. (1974). Rape trauma syndrome. American Journal of Psychiatry, 131, 981-986.

Burgess, A. W. & Holmstrom, L. L. (1979). Adaptive strategies in recovery from rape. American Journal of Psychiatry, 136, 1278-1282.

Burland, J. A. & Raskin, R. (1990). The psychoanalysis of adults who were sexually abused in childhood: A preliminary report from the discussion group of the American Psychoanalytic Association. In H. B. Levine (Ed.), Adult analysis and childhood sexual abuse (pp. 35- 41). Hillsdale, NJ: The Analytic Press.

Campbell, D. T. & Fiske, D. W. (1959). Convergent and discriminant validation by the multitrait-multimethod matrix. Psychological Bulletin, 56, 81-105.

Carmil, D. & Breznitz, S. (1991). Personal trauma and world view---Are extremely stressful experiences related to political attitudes, religious beliefs and future orientation? Journal of Traumatic Stress. 4, 393-405.

Carr, A. C. (1984). Intra-individual consistency in response to tests of varying degrees of ambiguity. Journal of Consulting Psychology, 18, 251-258.

Colson, D. (1982). Protectiveness in borderline states: A neglected object-relations paradigm. Bulletin of the Menninger Clinic, 46, 305-320.

Coons, P. M. (1980). Multiple personality: Diagnostic considerations. Journal of Clinical Psychiatry, 41, 330-336.

Cornett, C. (1985). The cyclical pattern of child abuse from a psychoanalytic self-psychology perspective. Child and Adolescent Social Work, 2, 83-92.

Crowne, D. P. & Marlowe, D. (1960). A new scale of social desirability independent of psychopathology. Journal of Consulting Psychology, 24, 349-354.

Doehring, C. (1987). A hall of mirrors: Dreams and therapy of violated women. Unpublished manuscript.

Doehring, C. (1993). The absent God: When neglect follows sexual violence. To be published in The Journal of Pastoral Care, 47.

Eagle, M. N. (1984). Recent developments in psychoanalysis. New York: McGraw-Hill.

Eisenman, R., Bernard, J. L., & Hannon, J. E. (1966). Benevolency, potency and God. Perceptual and Motor Skills, 22, 75-78.

Erikson, K. T. (1976). Everything in its path: Destruction of community in the Buffalo Creek disaster. New York: Simon & Schuster.

Fairbairn, R. (1952). The repression and the return of the bad objects (with special reference to the 'war neuroses'). In Psychoanalytic studies of the personality (pp. 59-81). London: Tavistock.

Ferenczi, S. (1932). Confusion of tongues between adults and children (The language of tenderness and the language of passion). In J. Masson (1985), The assault on truth (pp. 291-303). New York: Penguin.

Figley, C. R. (1986). Traumatic stress: The role of the family and the social support system. In C. R. Figley (Ed.), Trauma and its wake: Volume II (pp. 39-54). New York: Brunner/Mazel.

Figley, C. R. & Burge, S. K. (1983). Social support: Theory and measurement. Presented at the Groves Conference on Marriage and the Family. Freeport, Grand Bahamas Island.

Finkelhor, D. (1984). Child sexual abuse: New theory and research. New York: Free Press.

Fish-Murray, C. G., Koby, E. V., & van der Kolk, B. A. (1987). Evolving ideas: The effects of abuse on children's thought. In B. A. van der Kolk (Ed.), Psychological Trauma (pp. 89-110). Washington, DC: American Psychiatric Press.

Fortune, M. (1983). Sexual violence: The unmentionable sin. New York: Pilgrim Press.

Fortune, M. (1987). Keeping the faith: Questions and answers for the abused woman. San Francisco, CA: Harper & Row.

Fraiberg, S. (1975). Ghosts in the nursery: A psychoanalytic approach to the problems of impaired infant-mother relationships. Journal of the American Academy of Child Psychiatry, 14, 387-421.

Freud, A. (1936). The ego and the mechanisms of defense. In (1966) The writings of Anna Freud (Vol. 2). New York: International University Press.

Freud, A. (1967). Comments on trauma. In S. Furst (Ed.), Psychic Trauma (pp. 235-245). New York: Basic Books.

Freud, A. & Burlingham, D. (1944). Infants without families: The case for and against residential nurseries. New York: International University Press.

Freud, S. (1912). The dynamics of transference. In J. Strachey (Ed.), Freud's Completed Works (Vol. 12). London: Hogarth Press.

Freud, S. (1914a). Remembering, repeating and working through. In J. Strachey (Ed.), Freud's Completed Works (Vol. 12). London: Hogarth Press.

Freud, S. (1914b). Some reflections on schoolboy psychology. In J. Strachey (Ed.), Freud's Completed Works (Vol. 13). London: Hogarth Press.

Freud, S. (1917). Beyond the pleasure principle. In J. Strachey (Ed.), Freud's Completed Works (Vol. 18). London: Hogarth Press.

Freud, S. (1926). Inhibitions, symptoms and anxiety. In J. Strachey (Ed.), Freud's Completed Works (Vol. 20). London: Hogarth Press.

Friedrich, W. & Boriskin, J. (1976). The role of the child in abuse: A review of the literature. American Journal of Orthopsychiatry, 46, 580-589.

Gallup opinion index: Religion in America. (1981). Princeton, NJ: American Institute of Public Opinion.

Gediman, H. K. (1991). Seduction trauma: Complemental intrapsychic and interpersonal perspectives on fantasy and reality. Psychoanalytic Psychology, 8, 381-401.

Gelles, R. & Straus, M. A. (1988). Intimate violence: The definitive study of the causes and consequences of abuse in the American family. New York: Simon & Schuster.

General Social Survey. (1983). J.A. Davis (Principal Investigator). Chicago, IL: National Opinion Research Center.

Godin, A. & Coupez, A. (1957). Religious projective pictures: A technique of assessment of religious psychism. Lumen Vitae, 12, 260-274.

Godin, A. & Hallez, M. (1964). Parental images and divine paternity. In From religious experience to a religious attitude (pp. 79-110). Brussels: Lumen Vitae Press.

Gorsuch, R. L. (1968). The conceptualization of God as seen in adjective ratings. Journal for the Scientific Study of Religion, 7, 56-64.

Gottlieb, J. (1977). Multiple personality: A continuing enigma. Current Concepts in Psychiatry, January-February, 15-23.

Graham, L. K. (1992). Care of persons, care of the world: A psychosystems approach to pastoral care and counseling. Nashville, TN: Abingdon.

Green, A. H. (1978). Psychopathology of abused children. American Academy of Child Psychiatry, 17, 92-103.

Green, A. H. (1983). Dimensions of psychological trauma in abused children. Journal of the American Association of Abused Children, 22, 231-237.

Greenberg, J. R. & Mitchell, S. A. (1983). Object relations in psychoanalytic theory. Cambridge, MA: Harvard University Press.

Greven, P. (1990). Spare the child: The religious roots of punishment and the psychological impact of physical abuse. New York: Knopf.

Guntrip, H. (1969). Schizoid phenomena, object relations and the self. New York: International Universities Press.

Hammersla, J. F., Andrews-Qualls, L. C., & Frease, L. G. (1986). God concepts and religious commitment among Christian university students. Journal for the Scientific Study of Religion, 25, 424-435.

Harms, E. (1944). The development of religious experience in children. American Journal of Sociology, 50, 112-122.

Heinrichs, D. J. (1982). Our father which art in heaven: Paratoxic distortions in the image of God. Journal of Psychology and Theology, 10, 120-129.

Heise, D. R. (1965). Semantic differential profiles for 1000 most frequent English words. Psychological Monographs, 79, 31.

Heller, D. (1986). The children's God. Chicago: Chicago University Press.

Hendin, H. & Pollinger Haas, A. (1984). Combat adaptations of Vietnam veterans without post-traumatic stress disorder. American Journal of Psychiatry, 141, 956-960.

Hendin, H., Pollinger Haas, A., Singer, P., et al. (1983). The influence of precombat personality on post-traumatic stress disorders. Comprehensive Psychiatry, 24, 530-534.

Herman, J. (1992). Trauma and recovery. New York: Basic Books.

Herman, J., Perry, J. C. & van der Kolk, B. A. (1989). Childhood trauma in borderline personality disorder. American Journal of Psychiatry, 146, 490-495.

Herman, J. & van der Kolk (1990). Traumatic antecedents questionnaire. Personal correspondence.

Higdon, J. & Faheem, S. (1984). Fundamental religious upbringing as a contributing factor in a case with multiple personality. The American Atheist, December, 12-16.

Horowitz, M.J. (1976). Stress response syndromes. New York: Jason Aronson.

Horowitz, M. J., Wilner, N. & Alvarez, W. (1979). Impact of Event Scale: A measure of subjective stress. Psychological Medicine, 41, 209-218.

Hymer, S. (1984). The self in victimization: Developmental versus conflict perspectives. Victimology: An International Journal, 9, 142-150.

Imbens, A. & Jonker, I. (1992). Christianity and incest. (P. McVay, Trans.) Minneapolis, MN: Fortress Press.

Janoff-Bulman, R. (1985). The aftermath of victimization: Rebuilding shattered assumptions. In C. R. Figley (Ed.), Trauma and its wake (pp. 15-35). New York: Brunner/Mazel.

Janoff-Bulman, R. (1989a). Assumptive worlds and the stress of traumatic events: Applications of the schema concept. Social Cognition, 7, 113-136.

Janoff-Bulman, R. (1989b). The benefits of illusions, the threat of disillusionment, and the limitations of accuracy. Journal of Social and Clinical Psychology, 8, 158-175.

Janoff-Bulman, R. (1992). Shattered assumptions: Towards a new psychology of trauma. New York: The Free Press.

Jolley, J. C. & Taulbee, S. J. (1986). Assessing perceptions of self and God: Comparison of prisoners and normals. Psychological Reports, 59, 1139-1146.

Johnson, W. B. & Eastburg, M. C. (1992). God, parent and self concepts in abused and nonabused children. Journal of Psychology and Christianity, 11, 235-243.

Jordan, M. (1986). Taking on the Gods: The task of the pastoral counselor. Nashville, TN: Abingdon Press.

Justice, W. G. (1984). A comparative study of the language people use to describe the personalities of God and their earthly parents. Ann Arbor, MI: University Microfilms International.

Justice, W. G. & Lambert, W. (1986). A comparative study of the language people use to describe the personalities of God and their earthly parents. Journal of Pastoral Care, 40, 166-172.

Kendall-Tackett, K. A., Meyer Williams, L. & Finkelhor, D. (1993). Impact of sexual abuse on children: A review and synthesis of recent empirical studies. Psychological Bulletin, 113, 164-180.

Khan, M. (1963). The concept of cumulative trauma. The Psychoanalytic Study of the Child, 18, 286-306.

Klein, M. (1948). Contributions to psychoanalysis. London: Hogarth Press.

Kobasa, S. C., & Pucetti, M. C. (1982). Personality and social resources in stress resistance. Journal of Personality and Social Psychology, 45, 839-850.

Kohut, H. (1971). Analysis of the self. New York: International Universities Press.

Kohut, H. (1977). The restoration of the self. New York: International Universities Press.

Kohut, H. (1982). Introspection, empathy, and the semi-circle of mental health. International Journal of Psychoanalysis, 63, 395-407.

Kohut, H. (1984). How does analysis cure? Chicago, IL: University of Chicago Press.

Kohut, H. (1985). Self psychology and the humanities. C. B. Strozier (Ed.).
New York: Norton & Co.

Kohut, H. & Wolf, E. (1978). The disorders of the self and their treatment: An
outline. International Journal of Psychoanalysis, 59, 413-425.

Kowitt, M. P. (1985). Rorschach content interpretation in post-traumatic stress
disorders: A reply to Carr. Journal of Personality Assessment, 49, 21-24.

Krohn, A. & Mayman, M. (1974). Object representations in dreams and
projective tests. Bulletin of the Menninger Clinic, 38, 445-446.

Krugman, S. (1987). Trauma in the family: Perspectives on the intergenerational
transmission of violence. In B. A. van der Kolk (Ed.), Psychological
Trauma (pp. 127-151). Washington, DC: American Psychiatric Press, Inc.

Krystal, H. (1984). Psychoanalytic views on human emotional damages. In
B.A. van der Kolk (Ed.), Post traumatic stress disorder: Psychological and
biological sequelae. Washington D.C.: American Psychiatric Press.

Krystal, H. (1988). Integration and self-healing: Affect, trauma and alexithymia.
Hillsdale, NJ: The Analytic Press.

Kundera, M. (1988). The art of the novel. (L. Asher, Trans.) New York:
Grove Press.

Larsen, L. & Knapp, R. H. (1969). Sex differences in symbolic conceptions of
the deity. Journal of Projective Techniques and Personality Assessment, 28,
303-306.

Laufer, R. S., Brett, E. & Gallops, M. S. (1984). Post-traumatic stress disorder
reconsidered: PTSD among Vietnam veterans. In B. A. van der Kolk (Ed.),
Post-traumatic stress disorder: Psychological and biological sequelae.
Washington, DC: American Psychiatric Press.

Laufer, R.S., Frey-Wouters, E., & Gallops, M.S. (1985). Traumatic stressors
in the Vietnam war and post-traumatic stress disorder. In C. Figley (Ed.),
Trauma and its wake (pp.73-89). New York: Brunner/Mazel.

Levinson, D. (1989). Family violence in cross-cultural perspective. Newbury
Park, CA: Sage Publications.

Lidz, T. (1946). Nightmares and the combat neuroses. Psychiatry, 9, 37-49.

Lifton, R. J. (1976). The life of the self. New York: Simon & Schuster.

Lifton, R. J. (1979). The broken connection. New York: Simon & Schuster.

Lifton, R. J. (1988). Understanding the traumatized self: Imagery, symbolization, and transformation. In J. P. Wilson, Z. Harel, & B. Kahana (Eds.), Human adaptation to extreme stress: From the Holocaust to Vietnam (pp. 7- 31). New York: Plenum Press.

Lindy, J. D. (1986). An outline for the psychoanalytic psychotherapy of post-traumatic stress disorder. In C. R. Figley (Ed.), Trauma and its wake, Vol. II (pp. 195-212). New York: Brunner/Mazel.

Maier, S. F., & Seligman, M. E. P. (1976). Learned helplessness: Theory and evidence. Journal of Experimental Psychology, 105, 3-46.

Mayman, M. (1968). Early memories and character structure. Journal of Projective Techniques and Personality Assessment, 32, 303-316.

McCann, I. L. & Pearlman, L. A. (1990). Psychological trauma and the adult survivor: Theory, therapy and transformation. New York: Brunner/Mazel.

McDargh, J. (1983). Psychoanalytic object relations theory and the study of religion: On faith and the imaging of God. New York: University Press of America.

Meissner, W. W. (1977). The psychology of religious experience. Communio, 4, 36-59.

Meissner, W. W. (1978). Psychoanalytic aspects of religious experience. Annual of Psychoanalysis, 6, 103-141.

Meissner, W. W. (1984). Psychoanalysis and religious experience. New Haven, CN: Yale University Press.

Meissner, W. W. (1987). Life and faith: Psychological perspectives on religious experience. Washington, DC: Georgetown University Press.

Meissner, W. W. (1992). Religious thinking as transitional conceptualization. The Psychoanalytic Review, 79, 175-196.

Miller, A. (1986). Thou shalt not be aware: Society's betrayal of the child. New York: New American Library.

Mogenson, G. (1989). God is a trauma. Dallas, TX: Spring.

Muslin, H. L. (1985). Heinz Kohut: Beyond the pleasure principle, contributions to psychoanalysis. In J. Reppen (Ed.). Beyond Freud: A study of modern psychoanalytic theory (pp. 203-229). Hillsdale, NJ: The Analytic Press.

Nelsen, H. M., Cheek, N. H. Jr., & Au, P. (1985). Gender differences in images of God. Journal for the Scientific Study of Religion, 24, 396-402.

Nelsen, H. M., Waldron, T. W. & Stewart, K. (1973). Image of God and religious ideology and involvement: A partial test of Hill's southern culture-religion thesis. Review of Religious Research, 15, 37-44.

Nelson, M. O. (1971). The concept of God and feelings towards parents. Journal of Individual Psychology, 27, 46-49.

Nelson, M. O. & Jones, E. M. (1957). An application of the Q-technique to the study of religious concepts. Psychological Reports, 3, 293-297.

Osgood, C. E., Suci, G. J., & Tannenbaum, P. H. (1957). The measurement of meaning. Urbana, IL: University of Illinois Press.

Palombo, J. (1981). Parental loss and childhood bereavement. Clinical Social Work Journal, 9, 3-33.

Parson, E. R. (1988). Post-traumatic stress disorders: Theoretical and practical considerations in psychotherapy of Vietnam war veterans. In J. P. Wilson, Z. Harel, & B. Kahana (Eds.), Human adaptation to extreme stress: From the Holocaust to Vietnam (pp. 245-284). New York: Plenum Press.

Pasquali, L. (1981). The representation of God and parental figures among North American students. In A. Vergote & A. Tamayo (Eds.), The parental figures and the representation of God: A psychological and cross-cultural study (pp.169-184). The Hague: Mouton.

Piaget, J. (1945). Play, dreams, and imitations in childhood. New York: Norton.

Piaget, J. (1970). Genetic epistemology. New York: Columbia University Press.

Piaget, J. (1971). Psychology and epistemology: Towards a theory of knowledge. New York: The Viking Press.

Poling, J. N. (1991). The abuse of power: A theological problem. Nashville, TN: Abingdon.

Polkinghorne, D. (1983). Methodology for the human sciences: Systems of inquiry. Albany, NY: State University of New York Press.

Potvin, R. H. (1977). Adolescent images of God. Review of Religious Research, 19, 43-53.

Pynoos, R. S. & Eth, S. (1985). Developmental perspective on psychic trauma in children. In C. R. Figley (ed.), Trauma and its wake (pp. 36-52). New York: Brunner/Mazel.

Randour, M. L. & Bondanza, J. (1987). The concept of God in the psychological formation of females. Psychoanalytic Psychology, 4, 301-313.

Rizzuto, A. M. (1974). Object relation and the formation of the image of God. British Journal of Medical Psychology, 47, 83-99.

Rizzuto, A. M. (1976). Freud, God, the devil and the theory of object representation. International Review of Psychoanalysis, 31, 165.

Rizzuto, A. M. (1979). The birth of the living God. Chicago: The University of Chicago Press.

Roberts, C. W. (1989). Imagining God: Who is created in whose image? Review of Religious Research, 30, 375-386.

Roof, W. C. & Roof, J. L. (1984). Review of the polls: Images of God among Americans. Journal for the Scientific Study of Religion, 23, 201-205.

Rothstein, A. (Ed.). (1986). The reconstruction of trauma: Its significance in clinical work. Mew York: International Universities Press.

Rotter, J. B. (1966). Generalized Expectancies for internal versus external control of reinforcement. Psychological Monographs, 80, 1.

Russell, D. (1982). Rape in marriage. New York: Macmillan.

Salley, R. D. & Teiling, P.A. (1984). Dissociated rage attacks in Vietnam veterans: A Rorschach study. Journal of Personality Assessment, 48, 99-103.

Saltman, V. & Solomon, R.S. (1982). Incest and the multiple personality. Psychological Reports, 50, 1127-1141.

Sandler, J. & Rosenblatt, B. (1962). The concept of the representational world. Psychoanalytic Study of the Child, 17, 128-145.

Schafer, R. (1968). Aspects of internalization. New York: International Universities Press.

Schafer, R. (1976). A new language for psychoanalysis. New York: International Universities Press.

Sexton, A. (1975). The awful rowing toward God. New York: Houghton Mifflin.

Shengold, L. (1989). Soul murder: The effects of childhood abuse and depression. New Haven: Yale University Press.

Silver, S. M. (1986). An inpatient program for post-traumatic treatment: Context as treatment. In C. R. Figley (Ed.), Trauma and its wake: Volume II (pp. 213-231). New York: Brunner/Mazel.

Spero, M. H. (1992). Religious objects as psychological structures: A critical integration of object relations theory, psychotherapy, and Judaism. Chicago: The University of Chicago Press.

Spilka, B., Addison, J. & Rosensohn, M. (1975). Parents, self, and God: A test of competing theories of individual-religion relationships. Review of Religious Research, 16, 154-165.

Spilka, B., Armatas, P. & Nussbaum, J. (1964). The concept of God: A factor analytic approach. Review of Religious Research, 6, 28-36.

Stephenson, W. (1953). The study of behavior: Q-technique and its methodology. Chicago: University of Chicago Press.

Stierlin, H. (1970). The function of inner objects. International Journal of Psychoanalysis, 51, 371.

Stolorow, R. D. & Atwood, G. E. (1992). Contexts of being: The intersubjective foundations of psychological life. Hillsdale, NJ: The Analytic Press.

Strunk, O. Jr. (1959). Perceived relationships between parental and deity concepts. Psychological Newsletter, 10, 222-226.

Tabachnick, B. G. & Fidell, L. S. (1983). Using Multivariate Statistics. San Francisco, CA: Harper & Row.

Tamayo, A. & Desjardins, L. (1976). Belief systems and conceptual images of parents and God. The Journal of Psychology, 92, 131-140.

Tamayo, A., & Duga, A. (1977). Conceptual representation of mother, father, and God according to sex and field of study. The Journal of Psychology, 97, 79-84.

Terr, L. (1979). Children of Chowchilla: A study of psychic trauma. Psychoanalytic Study of Children, 34, 547-623.

Terr, L. (1983). Chowchilla revisited: The effects of psychic trauma four years after a school bus kidnapping. American Journal of Psychiatry, 140, 1543-1550.

Terr, L. (1990). Too scared to cry. New York: Harper-Collins.

Titchener, J. L. (1986). Post-traumatic decline: A consequence of unresolved destructive drives. In C. R. Figley (Ed.), Trauma and its wake, Vol. II (pp. 5-19). New York: Brunner/Mazel.

Tjart, D. & Boersma, F. J. (1978). A comparative study of religious values of Christian and public school eighth graders. Journal of Psychology and Theology, 6, 132-140.

Tolpin, P. (1983). Self psychology and the interpretation of dreams. In A. Goldberg (Ed.), The future of psychoanalysis: Essays in honor of Heinz Kohut (pp. 255-272). New York: International Universities Press.

Tracy, D. (1983). The foundations of practical theology. In D. Browning (Ed.), Practical theology (pp. 63-85). San Francisco, CA: Harper & Row.

Trible, P. (1984). Texts of terror: Literary-feminist readings of biblical narratives. Philadelphia, PA: Fortress Press.

Tuohy, A. L. (1987). Psychoanalytic perspectives on child abuse. Child and Adolescent Social Work, 4, 25-40.

Ulman, R. B. & Brothers, D. (1988). The shattered self: A psychoanalytic study of trauma. Hillsdale, NJ: The Analytic Press.

Urist, J. (1977). The Rorschach test and the assessment of object relations. Journal of Personality Assessment, 41, 3-9.

van der Kolk, B. A. (1985). Adolescent vulnerability to post-traumatic stress. Psychiatry, 20, 365-370.

van der Kolk, B. A. (1987). The psychological consequences of overwhelming life experiences. In B. A. van der Kolk (Ed.), Psychological Trauma (pp. 1-30). Washington, D.C.: American Psychiatric Press.

van der Kolk, B. A. (1988). The trauma spectrum: The interaction of biological and social events in the genesis of the trauma response. Journal of Traumatic Stress, 1, 273-290.

van der Kolk, B.A., Blitz, R., Burr, W., Sherry, S. & Hartmann, E. (1984). Nightmares and trauma: A comparison of nightmares after combat with lifelong nightmares in veterans. American Journal of Psychiatry, 141, 187-190.

van der Kolk, B. A. & Ducey, C. P. (1989). The psychological processing of traumatic experience: Rorschach patterns in PTSD. Journal of Traumatic Stress, 2, 259-274.

Vergote, A. (1988). Guilt and desire: Religious attitudes and their pathological derivatives. (M. H. Wood, Trans.) New Haven, CN: Yale University Press.

Vergote, A. (1981a). The parental figures: Symbolic functions and the medium for the representation of God. In A. Vergote and A. Tamayo (Eds.), The parental figures and the representations of God: A psychological and cross-cultural study (pp. 1-23). The Hague: Mouton Publishers.

Vergote, A. (1981b). Overview and theoretical perspective. In A. Vergote and A. Tamayo (Eds.), The parental figures and the representations of God: A psychological and cross-cultural study (pp. 185-225). The Hague: Mouton Publishers.

Vergote, A. & Tamayo, A. (Eds.). (1981). The parental figures and the representations of God: A psychological and cross-cultural study. The Hague: Mouton Publishers.

Wilmer, H. A. (1986). Combat nightmares: Toward a therapy of violence. Spring, 1986, 120-139.

Winnicott, D. W. (1953). Transitional objects and transitional phenomenon. International Journal of Psychoanalysis, 26, 2.

Winnicott, D. W. (1958). Collected papers: Through pediatrics to psychiatry. New York: Basic Books.

Winnicott, D. W. (1966). The maturational process and the facilitating environment. New York: International Universities Press.

Winnicott, D. W. (1971). Playing and reality. New York: Basic Books.

Wolf, E. K. & Alpert, J. L. (1991). Psychoanalysis and child sexual abuse: A review of the post-Freudian literature. Psychoanalytic Psychology, 8, 305-327.

Wootton, R. J. (1990). God-representation and its relation to object relations and defensive functioning. Ann Arbor: University Microfilms International (9105385).

Wright, J. W. (Ed.). (1990). The universal almanac. Kansas City, MO: Andrews & McMeel.

AUTHOR INDEX

SUBJECT INDEX